DON'T
THROW AWAY
TOMORROW

DON'T THROW AWAY TOMORROW

*Living God's Dream
for Your Life*

ROBERT H. SCHULLER

HarperSanFrancisco
A Division of HarperCollins*Publishers*

The excerpt in chapter 6 first appeared in *President's Newsletter,* November 1983, Phi Delta Kappa, Bloomington, Ind., and in Robert H. Schuller, *Tough Times Never Last, But Tough People Do!* (Thomas Nelson, 1983).

HarperCollins Web site: http://www.harpercollins.com
HarperCollins®, ®, and HarperSanFrancisco™ are
trademarks of HarperCollins Publishers, Inc.

FIRST EDITION

Library of Congress Cataloging-in-Publication Data is available upon request.

ISBN 0–06–056342–7

05 06 07 08 09 RRD(H) 10 9 8 7 6 5 4 3 2 1

This book is
dedicated
to
YOU

May God who knows your name and
your needs better than I bless you as
you turn these pages.

May you find joy, courage, and confidence
in all of your tomorrows.

Contents

∞

Contents

❦

ONE

Don't Throw
Away Your Tomorrow

Tomorrow is your best friend.

This is the first book I have written in the fourth quarter of my life. And I openly confess that I, the author, am preaching to myself. For my last book was my autobiography, published at the age of seventy-five, the wrap-up year of the first three quarters of my life. I thought it was time to retire from writing—I assumed I would have nothing new to add to the thirty-five books written with this hand. But the truth is quite the opposite. Three years into my fourth quarter, I am experiencing insights that are remarkably distinctive—yes, different from anything I've ever consciously encountered in my entire life.

Perspective—that's the key word to explain how living in the fourth quarter of life unveils insights never before experienced in the younger years. For the first three quarters of my life, I was driven by dreams. At the age of five, I had the dream to become a minister. That dream took twenty years of serious education—high school, college, graduate school in theology—twenty years! Then I had the dream of building a church that would impact the world with a positive healing faith. So, with five hundred dollars, my wife and I came to California, a super secular state, bringing a spiritual message of hope. Now, a half century later, we look at our work of over five decades and are shocked at what we honestly—and humbly—see. We are stunned at the sight! Buildings and grounds that today stand in a garden of peace. A spiritual home base for a televised church service seen by tens of millions around the globe and heard every week in the great languages of the world—English, Dutch, German, Russian, Arabic, Chinese—and still expanding.

How did this all happen? From nothing, something was born. How do we explain it? In simple terms—as I understand the process—I have always lived in the future. Call it "vision." For the past seventy-five years I have been dreaming my dreams of tomorrow. Did I miss out on living in the now? Did I miss out on the joy of living in the present? I don't know. I was always living in tomorrow. Today? This is the time to dream dreams and plan tomorrow. Tomorrow? That's when I do what I can and should do without procrastination. Tomorrow I move from a positive attitude to a new era of positive action. My notes to myself carry these acronyms:

D-I-N—Do it now! And M-I-H—Make it happen!

Of course, from time to time, celebrations called me out of my mental living in tomorrow, back to the *now* moment. Today—a wedding, an anniversary, the birth of a child, a plane to catch, a speech to give, a building to dedicate.

Today--but today is only twenty-four hours. Tomorrow? In my thinking, tomorrow seems to go on and on and on forever. Tomorrow? That is where my goals live, begging me to reach out to them. Tomorrow? That is where judgment waits to announce the winner, and I don't want to be the loser. I see it as the time between the dreaming and the arriving, and it might be twenty years, forty years, one hundred years. Life for me has been made up of a little of today and a lot of tomorrow. And yesterday? For most of the past fifty years I kept these words of Jesus under the glass top of my desk: "No man, having put his hand to the plough and looking back, is fit for the kingdom of God" (Luke 9:62).

It's past. It's history. Tomorrow is my future. But today I am going to celebrate.

I find myself stopped for a moment. I can't help looking back. I'm going to celebrate the fiftieth anniversary of dreaming and creating a ministry. Today, I'm forced to stop living in tomorrow and take time to look back and say thank you to God and to my friends, to whom, from today's perspective, I see I am so indebted.

"Oh, my gosh," I gasp. "The past—it is awesome." Have I been lucky? No, I've been blessed! I look back over fifty years of work. What do I see? What do I feel? Something I have never seen—or felt—before in my lifetime. Call it *perspective.*

In this illuminating light of the reality of perspective, I am living in the *now* as never before! It is time to celebrate anniversaries.

Today we celebrate the fiftieth anniversary of a church that grew from a small audience in a drive-in theater to an audience of tens of millions. Now they look, not through windshields of cars, but at television screens. They are sitting not on automobile seats but on sofas and beds, and they adjust the volume not on little speakers but on remote controls.

What, now, do I see looking back? What inner voices do I hear standing on this mountain peak?

I see the long path behind me, and I see what I've experienced—achieved through stress. Stress? Yes, always. Every day? Yes. But from this perspective, I see it as the stress of success. Positive stress! Work! Dream! Hold on! Never give up! Keep on believing! Set goals beyond goals! Think bigger! Think longer! Practice positive faith, and be prepared to live in a world of creative, constructive, redemptive *stress*.

I've lived in that world called stress all my life. I had to. It was my calling. And if I retired now, what would life be like? Stress-free? So-called stress-free living would produce new stresses I've never experienced before. Like the stress of boredom. I would miss the important telephone calls and the very important letters demanding my insight and my legal autograph. Would my name be dropped from the VIP list to be invited to parties, board, or meetings? *Perspective!* Now I hear a voice, "Welcome positive stress. Avoid all stress, and you will be on a new page called *death*. Welcome success stress, and stay on the path called *life.*" The inner voice is loud and clear.

DON'T THROW AWAY TOMORROW!

Who throws away their tomorrows? Every person—the child, the adolescent, the teenager, the young married couple, the middle-aged, the senior adult, the aged and retired, the winners and the losers, the healthy, the sick and suffering.

When do people throw away their tomorrows? When opportunities are passed by. When invitations to growth possibilities are rejected. When our plans are already made.

Why do we let great possibilities in our tomorrows fade quietly away? To answer that question, let me begin by sharing with you where I am coming from.

Living in this jubilee year, I see that all of my impossible dreams are today a beautiful reality. My mind races back to the year I accepted the call from Norman Vincent Peale's denomination to build a West Coast version of Peale's New York Collegiate Church, dated 1628 and started by Dutch Reformed colonists on the island they bought from Native Americans and named New Amsterdam. That church was already 148 years old in 1776, the birthday of America. Today, the New York church remains the oldest meeting place of the Protestant denomination with the longest continuous ministry in the United States.

This prestigious denomination issued a call to me to go to California and build a church in a new suburb springing up in the acres of orange groves. The date was January 1955. So I came with a calling to start a church from scratch; with two members, my wife and me; $500 cash to open a new church bank account; and, most important, a commitment to spend my whole life building one church that could impact the world. During these fifty years I had to purchase land, in five separate parcels, to accommodate the growing church. It expanded to forty acres, which are now all used in ministry by the church. It was the stress of success, as I was called to be not only the pastor but also the builder, the planner, the organizer, the developer, the financier, and yes, even the architect—much of which I had not trained for in seminary or college.

In *My Journey,* my autobiography, I told how much of this happened. The first ten acres cost $6,000 an acre. Walt Disney was building Disneyland a mile away, so the second ten acres a few years later cost $100,000 an acre. The third ten acres, some years later, would cost us nearly $1,000,000 an acre. The last ten acres, with forty private houses, would cost us well over a million dollars an acre. The last house alone would cost us one million dollars. Then we moved the houses and removed streets, power, and telephone poles to complete the forty-acre church gardens on which today stand four magnificent architectural facilities, world renowned in their design, done by gold-medal architects, Richard Neutra, Philip Johnson, and Richard Meier. What an honor to see the Crystal Cathedral included in the 2004 publication *Great Buildings of the World,* by the editors of *Time.* It is truly humbling to be recognized for our commitment to excellence, to read that the Crystal Cathedral is listed as "one of the world's most influential, inspiring, and astonishing structures." And it is used every day for ministries of hope, encouragement, and faith.

During these first fifty years I went to bed every night thinking about tomorrow. At each great event dedicating these new expanding ministries over five decades, my mind wasn't really in the present. Even when our television ministry celebrated its one-thousandth program, and all five living United States presidents appeared on the telecast, I only briefly enjoyed the now because I was already mentally working to meet tomorrow's demands.

Today, with a lifetime of work virtually finished, for the first time I feel free to *stop, look around,* and, yes, look back. Now I can see my life has never been in yesterday and never in today, but always in tomorrow. I was able to dream impossible dreams because I had a forty-year plan. And when those forty years were up, I was sixty-eight—past retirement according to our national standards—but my master plan was unfinished. So I had to keep my eye on tomorrow for another ten years. Had I retired at that time I would have thrown away ten years of tomorrows! That's 3,650 tomorrows, not counting leap years! Today, as I write these lines, those ten years have been lived, and now that I am seventy-eight years old, I have another ten-year plan. That's a future that makes life meaningful with my newest impossible dreams.

Impossible dreams at seventy-eight? Yes, for I've lived to prove that anything is possible if we never give up and never quit making plans to keep on keeping on for tomorrow.

• • •

Don't throw away tomorrow! Yes, live God's dream for your life. I pray I can help you as I have been helped by so many people this past half century!

Some years ago I was traveling with an associate, Mike Nason, who has been on staff for nearly forty years. On the plane we were studying our itinerary—about three pages detailing several events in upcoming cities. When I had finished reviewing a page of the itinerary that I thought summarized that day's events, I took the sheet of paper and crumpled it up to throw it away. Mike said, "That's tomorrow's page! Don't throw away tomorrow."

Wow! A light went on. I discovered a universal principle: *Don't throw away tomorrow.* That's so easy to do. Crumple the paper. Throw it away. Move to the next subject.

We throw away tomorrow when ideas come and we are not ready for them, so we move on. "I'll pass on this one," we say, not really knowing what doors to opportunity we're closing. We don't even give the idea serious attention.

We throw away tomorrow when challenges come or when problems hit us.

We throw away tomorrow when we get our priorities all mixed up and lose our vision.

When you get overwhelmed, don't throw away tomorrow. There's a wonderful Bible verse that holds the key for tomorrow: "Sanctify yourself"—which means get together with

God, and get your divine act together—"Sanctify yourself, because tomorrow the Lord will do wonders among you" (Joshua 3:5). Wow!

Why do people throw away tomorrow? Well, in some cases it's fatigue. They are tired. They've had enough. When you walk around the Crystal Cathedral campus or visit one of the countries of the world where you see the *Hour of Power* television program, you will see many of my dreams fulfilled. But behind those dreams there were the shadows, the times of waiting, the times when I wondered how it could possibly all work out. So I held on to the Bible verses, "Be not weary in well doing, for in due season we shall reap if we faint not" (Galatians 6:9). And from the Book of Job, "When He has tried me, I shall come forth as gold" (Job 23:10).

It's tempting on an anniversary to look back. That's okay. That's appropriate. But don't get hung up and stay there and miss tomorrow. The truth is, at that time we must learn to look to tomorrow. That is where it will all happen.

Others throw away tomorrow because of disappointments and rejections. They didn't get the raise they expected. Look at all the years they worked for the company, and who got the promotion? They did not.

Then there are broken promises that were made and never fulfilled.

The low returns on your investments were not what you expected. And the rewards, were they worth the risks? It is very normal and human to get disappointed. It's okay to become disappointed, but don't let disappointments take control of your head and your heart until you throw away your tomorrow.

It is easy to succumb to negative thinking and negative people. Add up the rejections, the failures, the setbacks, and you just want to throw away tomorrow. But remember this fundamental principle of possibility thinking: "Never make an irreversible negative decision in a down time."

What really happens when you throw away tomorrow? You surrender leadership of your life's destiny to fate, to forces, to past failures, to frowning faces that spill out negative predictions. "It won't work." "You don't have what it takes." "It's impossible." Then you lose confidence, and belief in yourself is infected with a fatal pessimism. You give up and throw tomorrow in the wastebasket. The negative thinkers around you win.

Why do people damage and destroy the possibility thinkers and the dreamers of great dreams? For lots of reasons. Jealousy. Ignorance. Cynicism. A basic attitude of obstructionism. Some people allow negative emotions to rule and reign in their lives.

How can you keep on keeping on with your hopes and dreams in this negative emotional environment?

1. Reread the title of a certain book: *Tough Times Never Last, but Tough People Do!* I wrote that book. I lived it. Millions of copies are out there. Never turn the management of your mood and your mind to obstructionists.

2. Now read every line on every page of this book.

3. Face your fears. Confront your challenges with a stubborn, positive attitude.

There is a quiet place in Hawaii where for over thirty years I've gone to draw inspiration and write many of my books. I am there now as I write these lines. Every morning I go out and take my morning exercise—a long, strong walk along the beach. And always, just ahead of me, I see this elderly, gray-haired, Japanese gentleman. He has obviously suffered a stroke. The right side of his body—arm and leg—is almost immobilized, but he can hold and use a cane in his right hand. His left hand swings forward and backward, up and down, to keep his balance. I see him coming slowly toward me. We meet, we exchange smiles. What a spirit shines through his determined face! He just will not, does not, give up and surrender his future to the challenge of a wounded body. I do not speak his language, but he understands English, and his face and eyes and cheeks all become one big beautiful smile when I stop and simply say, "Keep it up. God is blessing you." This has gone on for the past four years. He would have been defeated and probably dead long ago, but he has never thrown away his tomorrow.

Yes, there are many reasons why people throw away tomorrows. Some throw away tomorrow because of fear of failure. They just are afraid of taking risks. You have often heard me say, "If you're afraid of taking risks and you are not taking a risk, then you're not living this moment in the realm of faith." When you live by faith, you are running on the "risk track" because faith is what you need to move ahead when you can't be sure that it's going to work out the way you hoped and planned. Are you tempted to throw away tomorrow because of a fear of failure? Nothing causes more tomorrows to be thrown away than this fear.

Then, of course, there is the frustration of politics, which can cause you to throw away tomorrow's dreams. Anytime you get an idea, you need people to help you put it together. That is the beginning of an institution. When you create an institution, levels of authority and boundaries need to be established. If everybody owns it, nobody owns it. If everybody is responsible for it, nobody will be responsible. So great institutions require the establishment of power positions, and then politics enters. Politics can be very positive and helpful because it keeps an infrastructure in place, but if politics finds you voting on the wrong side, you can throw away tomorrow because you find there is too much debate and ego involved.

Why do people throw away tomorrow? For some it's because they find fulfillment. They win a prize. Maybe they win the lottery. Now they have enough, and they don't want to work anymore. They lose their vision. It's tempting. I have had more honors than I've deserved and more rewards than I expected. It can be tempting just to say, "Well, I'm going to retire." But what would I do then? Sit in a chair and watch TV? Don't let fulfillment throw away your tomorrow.

You've heard people say, "I've been there, done that." Be

very careful of that sentence. It's a potentially explosive negative claim that can shoot a hole through many new dreams that God has for you. Yes, I still have dreams for the tomorrows that God gives me. You and I must see fulfillment as a broadening of the base of strength that will enable us to think in bigger dimensions than we have ever thought before!

Why do people throw away tomorrow? Of course, a shortfall of resources is a main reason. You don't have the money, and you can't see where it would come from. A lack of resources may slow you down, but don't let it make you throw away a big idea. Give God five years, ten years, fifteen years, twenty years, twenty-five years, thirty years, forty years, or more. Give God all the time He needs to bring the resources to you! Give God time—and the people, the craftsmen, the skill, the new inventions, the money will come. Don't throw away tomorrow.

Recently I was in Florida for a conference, so I stopped to see a friend from the television ministry. I visited him at his work and discovered that he is a banker. In fact, he owns this bank, a small one, and it's his second bank. As a young man he took a job as a janitor in the bank. He cannot claim exciting academic credentials. Nor can he claim that he knows powerful and rich people. But he is a possibility thinker. He has read my possibility thinking books, and he embraces a positive faith that he says helped him dare to believe he could make his dreams for tomorrow come true. When he was a janitor in the bank, a wild, impossible idea came into his brain: *Why don't you create your own bank? You can become CEO, become the president. All you need is the right ideas.* So he took the leap of faith, and he founded a bank with $3 million that he collected here and there. It was amazing how he managed to put that all together when he didn't start out with the money or the resources. The bank grew, and he sold it for a very good profit, and now he's building his second bank, where he is the executive officer. I met all of his top employees, fourteen of them. They are mostly young people who have been with him for ten years, twelve years, fourteen years; they love him. He treats them so generously that they don't want to work anywhere else. He is a positive-thinking believer, and he applies it in his business, in his ideas, and in his day-to-day work with his employees. Wow!

If you're tempted to see only the shortfall, remember, God often doesn't give you what you need until you've stuck your feet in the water. It was when Moses put his feet in the water and Pharaoh's army was coming down to capture and kill him that the Red Sea parted and Moses and the people of Israel walked across to freedom! Don't throw away tomorrow! Get faith, and let go of the doubt. Get into positive thinking, and do away with that negative thinking. Get into possibility thinking: *It might be possible if . . . It might be possible when . . . It might be possible with . . . It might be possible after . . . It might be possible, however . . .* But don't ever use that word *impossible!* Wow!

• • •

With God, there's always a tomorrow. Adam and Eve blew it, and God watched them walk out of the Garden in disgrace, losing their pride, their self-respect, their self-esteem. They walked out of the Garden humiliated and dishonored. And as God watched them, God planned a tomorrow!

Then there was the flood, but God, through Noah, planned a tomorrow. And God designed a rainbow, with His promise that if you are going through a flood, and if you don't throw away tomorrow, you are going to have some wonderful surprises that you couldn't have expected during the storm.

Believers around the world celebrate Easter. That's the tomorrow God planned for His people. We all need a vision of tomorrow, and when tomorrow comes we must grasp it. Saturate your mind with positive thinking. Negative thinking will produce what it promises—nothing. Positive thinking will produce something, and life will be better for others and for you! And something will always win over nothing.

Tomorrow, God will work wonders among you!

TWO

Start and Succeed
with Optimism

Positive thinking plus *possibility thinking* equals *optimism!*

To live God's dream for your life, you must have an optimistic attitude. Pessimists are afraid of tomorrow. Optimists never throw away tomorrow. You will need both positive thinking and possibility thinking to achieve fulfillment.

"Why," I'm often asked, "do I seem to alternate between positive thinking and possibility thinking? Is there a difference?" In my faith and my philosophy there is a difference.

It is the difference between attitude and action.

Positive thinking comes first. It is a *positive mental attitude that replaces a negative mental attitude or a lethargic mental attitude.* Positive thinking sets the stage. Your dream is conceived, but at this point it is still only wishful thinking. To go forward, your mind must evolve from positive thinking into possibility thinking.

In possibility thinking, the mental maneuvering moves from *attitude* ideas to *action* ideas. We make a commitment to create ways and means to make the dream come true in reality.

Positive thinking asks the question, "*Is* it possible?" Possibility thinking asks the "get-ready-to-get-going" question, "*How* can I make it happen?"

Possibility thinking puts wings and legs on positive ideas.

But at the heart and soul of both positive and possibility thinking is the same powerful optimism. Optimism is the all-empowering attitude that unfailingly delivers the energy to:

- Start.

- Stay with it, or

- Bounce back and start over again after disappointments.

Stephanie, my teenage granddaughter, reminded me of all the times I'd said to her, "What dreams would you have if you *knew* you would not fail?"

"Grandpa," she asked, "didn't you ever think you might fail?"

"Oh, yes," I answered. "I often faced the reality that I might fail, but I never *knew* that I *would* fail unless I failed to *try*. I could never be an optimist if I didn't risk failure. I *know* that if I face failure, I can turn it around and inside out, so that even a failure turns into a valuable positive experience. Stephanie, all through life you will find yourself in different circumstances, and you will need to choose whether you are going to be a pessimist or an optimist. I choose to be an optimist."

Sincere cynics often ask me, "How can you be optimistic in a world infected with pain and problems?"

"I am addicted to optimism," I answer. "I am basically a person with positive emotional charge. I make choices that hold the promise of creating more positive memories in my memory bank. My expanded positive memory system creates a feedback loop, generating more positive emotions, such as enthusiasm, hope, and faith. These happy, hopeful feelings make me feel strong. They assure me that I have the power to be creative through the best and worst times."

Beyond the power that it delivers to the subconscious, beyond the enthusiasm that it releases through a personality, and beyond the energy that it generates, optimism attracts other positive people to us. Their friendship and support add another protective layer to help us get through tough times. Positive people shun the pessimists but are attracted to the optimists. They want to be a part of the optimistic person's projects and dreams.

When pessimism takes command in a life or a family, in an organization or an institution, thoughts of failure seep in and fatigue begins to take over. Pessimism saps energy and makes you feel old. Pessimism drives positive people away.

Pessimism is the toxic soil where worry, fear, and anxiety sprout and choke life's dreams. Yes, pessimism chokes faith, pollutes positive thinking, and lets great dreams waste away in depression. What a pity. As Norman Cousins said, "Does anybody know enough to be a pessimist?"

One of the most inspiring women I have met has every reason to be a pessimist, but she chose to be an optimist instead.

Renee Bondi was a beautiful, energetic, intelligent twenty-nine-year-old, excited about both her singing career and her engagement to be married. She had the world at her fingertips, with multiple options and a promising future. Then one night a freak accident changed everything:

"One Sunday night," she reported, "I went to bed about 11:00 P.M. after what was a very ordinary, fun weekend. I had been dancing all night with my fiancé. I went to bed feeling great. The next thing I knew, I woke up about 2 A.M., diving off the end of my bed onto my head. When I hit my head on the ground, I heard my neck go *click-click-click*, and I finished the flip lying flat on my back. I had broken my neck.

"To this day we have absolutely no idea what happened. I don't have a history of sleepwalking or any disease that would cause a seizure. I broke my neck, and my life changed literally overnight."

Fortunately, Renee did not have to lie on the floor long before she received help from her roommate, who mysteriously awoke and went to Renee's room to "see if Renee was okay"! Renee credits this to God's providence—an amazing statement in and of itself. Many people would look toward God with bitterness after such an accident. Yet because of her faith in God's care for her, Renee chose a positive mental reaction.

"Who gets paralyzed falling out of bed?" she asked with the same amazement we all feel when we hear her story. "I didn't realize I was paralyzed, so as I went to get back in bed, this pain pierced my neck. I tried to holler for my roommate, and all that came out was a whisper. I thought, *Oh, my goodness, there's no way she's going to find me. She's sound asleep.* But literally within a couple of minutes the door opened and the light went on. My roommate was awakened out of a sound, deep sleep. I believe very strongly that the Holy Spirit woke her up."

Renee soon found out that the doctors' prognosis was bleak. "You are a quadriplegic—paralyzed from the neck down," they told her. "You'll never have use of your legs, and you'll never again have functional use of your arms or your fingers."

As Renee listened to the neurologists and neurosurgeons, denial seemed to be the only way to cope with the devastating news. It wasn't until she tried to sing again that the reality of her situation came crashing down on her.

"I was in the hospital for five months when a good friend of mine, a musician, came to visit me. He came in with a big smile and said, 'Renee, I found a piano in the dining room. Let's go.' So I went with him down the hallway in my wheelchair. Jim sat down at the piano and started playing. I tried to sing. Every time I tried to sing, I kept getting dizzy. I started to black out. I couldn't sing. I started crying. My friend got up, dumped his head on my shoulder, and we just sobbed. I realized that the very expression of who I was, which was my music, had also been taken away from me. It was devastating."

Renee's family filled the gap in her emotional needs as she went from being an independent woman to a person dependent on others for the most basic elements of life.

"My siblings and my mom and dad brought real special gifts to the table," she said. "Things like my dad welding a cup holder to be attached to my wheelchair so I could have the fluids that I needed every day. My sisters and my brother providing my medical needs so that I would stay healthy, so that I wouldn't die. My mom doing my laundry and tailoring my clothes so that they'd fit just perfectly when I sat in the chair. My students and their parents having great fund-raisers enabling me to purchase a wheelchair-accessible van. And of course, my fiancé always by me to make sure I felt comfortable in the wheelchair, making me smile. All these things lifted me up and gave me the strength."

And her positive Christian faith gave her the strength to remain optimistic. "I continued to pray during those really dark days, weeks, and months," she remembered. "I was able to see how God, through my family and all these people, was really the strength. They were God's hands helping me. It was the Lord, through them, saying, 'Be not afraid. I go before you always.'"

This support gave Renee the ability to work hard in physical therapy. Her voice, which was at first only a whisper, slowly became stronger. As her voice became stronger, so did her spirit.

"A couple of years later, again with the same friend, I tried to sing." She continued: "Sure enough, here came my voice. *I was singing.* Now I know that the strength came from the Lord."

Today Renee enjoys the fruits of her optimism. Her voice fills the entire Crystal Cathedral as she performs regularly for our services. She still has only partial movement in her arms and remains a quadriplegic. Yet she is married and has a son, whom she delivered naturally. She has recorded numerous albums and sings the most inspiring songs. Her optimism overflows and truly is contagious.

Optimism or pessimism. It's your choice. Expect the best and you may get it. Expect the worst and you may get *that*.

Why am I an optimist?

1. *I am an optimist because I believe in a cosmic power that is intelligent and compassionate.* God has given me a mission, and He has a mission for you too. That mission is my reason for living. It fills my life with meaning. It makes me alive with hope for the life waiting to be unfolded in the future. Yes, my faith in God gives me a divine imagination to envision a fruitful future filled with surprises of success.

   This vision of a positive future flows back in a cycle bringing even greater optimism.

   I was born into a strong Christian family. In my earliest years I was led to believe that there was Supreme Intelligence and a supremely affectionate core of divine reality in the spiritual universe. I was led to believe that this was "God" and that He had a plan for my life. "I have a plan for your life, a plan to give you a future with hope" (Jeremiah 29:11). I knew that if I followed God's plan, He would unfold it in my imagination. He would not let me fail. "He who has begun a good work in you will complete it" (Philippians 1:6).

We live in a material universe, but I also believe we live in a spiritual universe with a Higher Power that has a purpose for all life in creation: plant and animal, fowl and fish, insects and microbes. All of life is ecologically integrated. And the human being alone has the divine gift of creative imagination—even the capacity to imagine the invisible intelligent life form we call God.

2. *I am an optimist because I believe every person is important.* Every person is a force in his or her own world, with the capacity to influence surrounding people. Each person makes a difference to someone. Every positive person makes life better for those in his or her world. That gives enormous potential value to every life. "I have value" provides a powerful philosophical base for optimism.

All persons have enormous value when they are connected with God. Early in my ministry, intelligent people who were not religious often scorned the idea that one God could connect with every single person on earth. But today, when that population has swelled to six billion, we understand that a computer chip the size of a stamp or coin can connect six billion bits of information. I no longer find intelligent scientists who ask me, "How can one God connect with six billion people?"

3. *I am an optimist because I am positive that the sun will rise tomorrow.* I believe there is a future for us. That gives me the power to choose to greet the rising sun with hope, because there has never before in history been another day like tomorrow will be.

Babies will be born tomorrow, and as long as one new person is coming into the human family, there is no reason for anyone to be a total pessimist.

4. *I am an optimist because I know that whatever happens tomorrow, I can make a hopeful, helpful difference.* It's what I call "the power of one"—the power of one idea! the power of one decision! the power of one person!

History is always shaped by one person with a vision. A few, then more, and finally many people are inspired, and a movement is born. One person with an impassioned dream can change the world.

5. *I am an optimist because I see positive possibilities in every problem.* Charles F. "Boss" Kettering, an inventor at General Motors, said to his colleagues, "Problems are the price of progress. Don't bring me anything but trouble. Good news weakens me."

I was a teenager when I memorized this Bible verse: "All things work together for good to those who love God and keep His commandments" (Romans 8:28).

My profession has been to minister as a pastor-counselor to people facing problems, turmoil, suffering, and pain. For over fifty years, as an optimist, I have been helping people work through what they call problems. These problems have always turned out to be positive possibilities in disguise to persons who work their way from positive thinking, through possibility thinking, to unquenchable optimism.

Problems are never real problems unless they cause you to take your eye off your goals. When a negative reaction threatens you, look over and beyond the problem. Give God time to work it out. Keep the faith, and you'll be surprised how your "problem" delivers unexpected blessings.

Problems never become real problems *until* and *unless* we stop believing that God loves us.

I have counseled thousands of people who went "through the valley" and unanimously have said, "Looking back, I wouldn't want to change the hard times. My scar has become a star!"

6. *I am an optimist because I have come to believe that all problems are illusions.* Whatever you do, don't throw away tomorrow because of problems still left to be solved, resolved, or managed. *All problems are really decisions.* They are often the stimulus to make new decisions today that will correct the mistakes you made yesterday.

Yes—many problems are decisions that we have yet

to make. The reason we call them problems is that we don't want to make decisions, or we are afraid of making new and challenging decisions. When we confront the challenge with optimism, then we change the shape or the scope of that "problem," allowing us to survive and thrive in the new tomorrows that are certain to be born.

"But, Dr. Schuller," a problem-burdened listener said to me, "you're in denial when you say that problems don't exist and they're really decisions. What's the difference?"

There is a huge difference. Using the word *problem* implies that the conditions are out of your control. That negative perception paralyzes positive thinking as well as possibility thinking. But if problems are, in reality, decisions waiting to be made, then the awesome, immeasurable power of the human spirit can be released in a redemptive reaction. And you and I always—yes, *always*—have the freedom to decide. "What will I allow this 'problem' to do to my spirit?" you can ask. "I have the freedom to choose how I will react to this pain," you can say. "I can make the positive decision to turn my pain into gain, and an obstacle into an opportunity."

7. *I'm an incurable optimist because the attitude of optimism has always increased my odds of success—and always will.* I have crossed the continents and countries of planet earth many times. Through television, books, and lectures, I

have communicated with hundreds of millions of people for well over thirty-five years. I have lived seventy-eight years and hope to reach one hundred, and here is what I've learned:

God is alive in every corner of the earth. I always "see God alive" through the loving, beautiful people I find anywhere in the world. Out there, everywhere, are people who are sensitive to human problems and pain. Instinctively, they sense the pain and peril in the human family and are swift to move in and help hurting people.

"I would have lost heart unless I had believed that I would see the goodness of the Lord in the land of the living" (Psalm 27:13). There is a Divine Spirit loose in the world that will be there when we need it. Hospitals, schools, peacekeepers. Courts administering justice. Caregiving institutions. The Red Cross. The Salvation Army. World Vision. Houses of worship and positive, optimistic movements. I am incurably optimistic that help will come out of nowhere from people I've never met before.

8. *I am an optimist because love outweighs hatred in the human family.* The first experience for almost every newborn baby is love. We are born in love. We have to learn to hate.

If you cannot sense and feel the Universal Spirit of Love that is alive all over the world, then you are not mixing with positive-thinking people, reading the right kind of books, and, yes, attending a positive, loving place of worship.

9. *I'm addicted to optimism because even in the most pessimistic climates, there are always alternatives and options.* Pessimism is surrendering leadership to negative assumptions. Pessimism drops the curtain on tomorrow. Pessimism cuts off any hope of a prosperous future. Pessimism predicts and delivers a debilitating destiny.

We must never forget that we humans are "A and O" people: A for Alternatives, O for Options. When pain and peril challenge us, we can create alternatives. Optimism refuses to believe that the road ends without options.

When there are no options, we create options! When we face apparent defeat, we find a detour or build a bridge.

Because the world is in constant change, new options will be open to us tomorrow that may not be open to us today. Rejected yesterday? Go back—a new person, with a new attitude, may be at the desk! What a difference one day—and one new person —can make.

So when pessimism drops the curtain on tomorrow, optimism raises it back up. We see new doors opening tomorrow that were never open before!

All of us can position ourselves to see the future with optimism and hope. And that happens only as we exercise faith, because optimism and enthusiasm don't just drop out of the sky. Optimism is not something you can eat or drink. It's something that bubbles up from the depths of your own heart and soul. It comes when you exercise leadership over your own life and your own destiny.

10. *I'm addicted to optimism because I have seen in my lifetime the awesome power of the human spirit.* I have always been inspired by Jesus Christ, how He illustrated in His own life that the human spirit can face and overcome human suffering. Jesus died on a cross in pain and shame, yet He did not for a moment give in to hatred. "Father, forgive them" was His reaction. He was an optimist to the end. He looked ahead with hope. With faith in a positive God, we can do the same. We can come from nowhere and go anywhere. We can shine like a bright inspiring light as we live and move on through the dark times of life, facing the worst that life throws at us.

Every human being who disciplines himself to hold on to faith in days of disaster will endure and find himself embraced with affection and respect by the best people in his time and world.

The human being has an awesome power of spirit to embrace life. With humans like that in our world, we can all be optimists.

11. *I'm an optimist because I believe we can always choose new positive and beautiful dreams that will come true again and*

again. Our hopes for tomorrow can become achievements. We can prove to a cynical world that optimists are the ultimate winners! Because optimists never accept failure as the last word, we turn failure into a bend in the road—*not* the end of the road. Optimists never use the two-word sentence "I quit." Only God is allowed that move.

12. *I choose to be an optimist because I have been inspired by so many other optimists in my life.* We seem to be drawn to each other as we seek out those who know that optimism works wonders.

Many incredible optimists have shared their stories of overcoming the odds with a can-do spirit. One woman, a true optimist, stands out: the television series *Sue Thomas: F.B.Eye*, on the Fox station, is based on her life and shows a fictional version of a true-life wonder. Sue Thomas has shared her incredible story at the Crystal Cathedral more than once. What an inspiration she has been as she shared how her faith has sustained her optimistic attitude despite tremendous challenges.

"Basically, I was too young to remember," Sue said. "But at eighteen months of age, I sat in front of the TV with my three older brothers. At a given moment, I went and turned the volume up full blast. My brothers ran up and turned it down. I turned it up again, and they turned it down. Mom and Dad came running to find out what all the ruckus was about, and they thought that I was getting tired and cranky. It was time to put me to bed. That night when my parents tucked me into bed, neither of them realized that it would be the very first long silent night of the rest of my life.

"It wasn't until morning that my mom realized I was totally oblivious to my surroundings and she grew concerned. She called our neighbor, who was a nurse, and after a lot of discussion I was rushed to the hospital. There the doctors examined me and turned to my parents and said those words that would follow them the rest of their lives: 'There's no hearing. She's profoundly deaf.'"

Sue's parents immediately led the way in their daughter's optimism training by refusing to allow her to be institutionalized, which was the common practice with deaf children at the time. Instead, they believed she could live a normal life, and they gave her the tools to help her do so.

Today when Sue speaks before audiences, her speech is as clear as a hearing person's. Her diction is perfect, and her ability to read the lips of the people around her is amazing.

When she was a child, however, her deafness made her a target for other children. They ridiculed this hearing-impaired young girl who couldn't talk correctly. So Sue escaped to the skating rink. As a result, at the age of seven she became the youngest freestyle champion in Ohio's skating history.

Sue also focused on her goal to learn to speak correctly. It was achieved, she believes, with help from others.

"By God's grace, there was a lot of dedication from my parents and speech therapists. For years I sat in front of a very large mirror with my speech therapist by my side, and she would begin to speak and take my hand and put it on her throat so that I could feel the vibrations. Then I was to put my hand on my own throat and feel those same vibes. In front of the mirror I would watch how she would form her mouth, and I was to try to form my mouth the same way.

"It was during all those years in front of the mirror that I gained the skill of reading lips. It wasn't intentional at the very beginning. It just came about as a gift. I also had years of voice lessons to get my voice to fluctuate up and down, up and down, and then I had a year of dramatic reading in poetry with an English teacher, to learn to recite word for word with articulation and enunciation.

"In spite of all these efforts, I know I still talk just a little bit different. I'll be at an airport, at a hotel or restaurant, and somebody will always come up and say to me, 'Ma'am, where are you from? You really have an accent.'"

Sue's optimistic, healthy approach despite her disability earned her a bachelor's degree in 1976. Her hard work paid off when she was hired by the Federal Bureau of Investigation in Washington, D.C., to be a fingerprint examiner.

"They were hiring deaf people to search and classify fingerprints," she explained. "They felt that if a person couldn't hear, there wouldn't be any distractions. So I had to be able to detail all those funny lines on people's fingerprints eight hours a day, five days a week."

One day God rewrote that chapter of Sue's story. "The agents came to me and began to ask me a lot of questions:

'Do you watch TV?' 'Is it difficult for you?' 'Do you go to the movies?' Finally they shared with me that they had a problem. They had videotaped a suspect, but when the camera activated, the sound mechanism failed. They had all this film with people talking, but they couldn't hear it. They wanted to know if I could watch it and write down the words. I said, 'Sure, no problem.' From that day on I never went back to reading fingerprints. I went on to read lips for the FBI."

Her time at the FBI led to the TV series about her life, but it is clear that Sue Thomas is not content with simply having television retell her story. She is very busy concentrating on her future. She has continued to build on her success in living an extraordinary life despite challenges. And the challenges have continued.

"Sixteen months ago I was diagnosed with MS—multiple sclerosis. My eyesight has deteriorated, my walking has slowed, and my balance is out of whack. I've come to understand the word *grace* with each passing day God gives me. Because He lives, I can indeed face tomorrow."

Sue Thomas has continued to amaze me with her optimistic faith. "My parents taught me at a very early age that there was a God and I was created in His image; that He had a Son so powerful that as long as I kept my hands in His and allowed Him to lead and guide me through life, there couldn't be anything I couldn't do or become. I walked with Him as a child. He has been my rock. Just when I think I know Him,

He takes me on a completely new journey where I gain understanding of Him in a deeper, more profound way.

"I have a certified hearing dog for the deaf that alerts me to all sounds: when the doorbell goes off, the smoke detector, a baby crying, all those things. My dog will find me and lead me to where the sound is. She has given me my independence back. God uses all of His creatures great and small to accomplish His will. If He can use this dog so powerfully to transform and change my life, how much more can He use people if we allow Him?"

Today Sue's message, both through a television series and her personal appearances, is one of enormous encouragement to others facing incredible challenges.

"I want to bring hope to people: for parents dealing with a child who has physical problems or may just be at a difficult stage. With tough love, if they stay with that child, in the end it will work out. For every child who has been an outcast, ridiculed, made fun of—hang tough. It won't always be this way. There is a tomorrow, and it will be brighter. To every deaf educator, speech therapist, or those in the medical profession, I say, never give up with a person you are working with. Someday you will see the wonderful final result."

Choose to be an optimist, and you will so live that when you die you'll leave behind a life far more inspiring than that of any pessimist. I'd rather be an optimist who overestimated his success than a pessimist who fulfilled his gloomy prediction. For the journey of the optimist is a joyful trip, and the journey of the pessimist is a trip lived every day without the energy of hope enlightening every tomorrow. When you believe in a positive, loving God, as Sue Thomas does, there isn't anything you can't do or become.

Never throw away tomorrow!

Now—find God's dream for your life and go all out for it!

∽

THREE

Discover and
Determine Your Mission

Everyone needs a mission that will give purpose and
meaning to life.

His caricature is as famous as his name. The broad fore-head swooping down to a long nose on the upswing, followed by a mouth caught in a hearty laugh. His customary "Thanks for the memories" underscored his enthusiasm for life. But on July 27, 2003, at the age of one hundred, Bob Hope passed away.

I knew Bob Hope—he was my friend, and I was honored to be included in the funeral procession at his memorial mass.

What made Bob Hope such a legendary entertainer? Was it that his joy and laughter brought relief to the weary? Was it the hope he found and shared through humor? Or was it the selfless service he took upon himself to bring Christmas wishes to American troops stationed in war zones throughout the world? Yes—it was all these things and more. He was a perennially optimistic man on a lifelong mission.

Bob Hope was unselfishly driven by a calling to bring healthy humor into the world. Many times I witnessed him at benefits, selflessly taking the time out of his dinner to be photographed with fans. He always had time for charity events. He taught millions of people, including his own children, about the gift of giving.

Now, I'm not suggesting that your calling is to become a celebrity like Bob Hope. But I am making this point: there must be a compelling purpose and mission in your life. We all need to know that we can and will make a difference.

The human spirit has an inextinguishable hunger for a cause so consuming that it can fill the emptiness of the soul with pride, purpose, and pleasure.

The late Viktor Frankl called this sense of purpose, both passionate and practical, the "meaning" in life. As a Jew in the Nazi death camps, he realized his mission was first to survive, and then to use his professional psychiatric counseling skills to serve the other suffering and dying inmates. He saw this as his divine calling, his mission. This mission gave him a purpose in living and kept him alive with dignity in spite of horrific conditions.

The first rule of optimistic living is this: prepare a positive personal mission statement that will turn your dreams into definite goals. A goal-less life is a God-less life.

My mission statement keeps me focused on the meaning

and purpose of my life and helps me to stay on course through the evolving challenges and accomplishments of this process called living.

Far too many people live without a clear, consuming mission. Instead of an inner drive flowing from the force of a focused faith, they have an inner lethargy that makes for an aimless existence. Their personal behavior is shaped by reactivity instead of proactivity. The energy generated by commitment is missing from their lives. Instead, life for them is vague, unfocused, and indecisive.

At university graduation exercises the young people look so confident in their caps and gowns, yet in every class there are many graduates who are uncertain about where they will go from there. They have seen the diploma as an end in itself, not as preparation for launching their life's mission. No wonder we find college graduates taking a job in a retail store and explaining their confusion with the simple defense, "I haven't found my calling yet."

I have had countless encounters with people who have a dull look in their eyes because they lack the inner passion and spirit that could promote and propel them with enthusiasm into a promising future. The truth is that no person is prepared for the engagement of living until he has found a cause or a calling that he can call his mission in life.

"What do you want to do in life?" I asked one of my grandson's friends visiting our home. The young high school student answered with the same response I have heard hundreds of times from young, bright, beautiful people.

JM: I don't know.

RHS: What are your talents and gifts?

JM: I don't have any special talents or gifts.

RHS: I see many gifts in you that I believe are special.

JM: Like what?

RHS: You can see. You can hear. You can think. You can touch. You can laugh. The first ten minutes in our casual conversation, I liked you a lot. Your personality is pleasant. You seem like a really great kid.

JM: Okay, but that makes me just an ordinary kid. I'm not gifted or talented. I can't sing. I can't dance. I can't act. I am not an athlete. I didn't even make the basketball team. I'm just an average kid.

RHS: It sounds like you are suffering from a cultural distortion of your self-image.

JM: What is that?

RHS: That means you appraise yourself more on "doing" than on "being." Which is more important? Gifts and talents in the quality of your personhood or your performance as an actor or athlete?

JM: I guess the kind of person I am.

RHS: Of course it's the person you are, for that is where relationships are formed and friendships are bonded; that's where love, trust, and respect are rooted. You have the natural gifts that can be respected, reverenced, and sharpened in skill and spirit. You can be the person who listens, who encourages, who motivates, whose smile brings energy into a room when you arrive and leaves a blessing when you depart. *Don't downplay your potential!* Become a positive person first, and your performance will follow. Don't fail to see the possibility in your personhood as a gift. Don't trivialize your treasure. Watch out for the tempting, seductive allure in American culture, shaped by the media.

JM: (*shrugs shoulders*)

RHS: You may not realize it, but I see an emerging spirit of hope and adventure in your eyes. Catch it, engage it. And by the way, I noticed you used a bad four-letter word. Cut it out. Never use it again.

JM: I didn't use a bad four-letter word. I never do. What did I say?

RHS: You said "just." That's a put-down word. Never use it. It belittles you. "I'm just a B student," "I'm just an average guy."

The single most systemic toxicity in a human personality is a negative self-image. It deprives you of your necessary sense of mission.

No person is "just" a performer. Each role is all-important! It is the optimistic person with a positive mission and a positive self-image who makes the greatest contribution to society.

The famed architect Mies van der Rohe made famous the wise expression "God is in the details." When van der Rohe commissioned an architectural student to design a building with an entire wall made up of bricks, he ordered the student not to simply sketch a portion of the wall but to depict each brick and every inch of mortar in it. The amount of mortar determines how many bricks are used, which affects the entire design and size of not only the wall but the entire building.

Applying this universal principle to the social architecture of relationships, you have probably noticed that when a celebrity enters a gathering, there are stares, whispers, and oohs and aahs. But you have probably also noticed that when a simple, sweet, caring person who is known as good, honest, and kind enters the circle, out come the hugs and happy hellos. With this kind of awareness, you'll begin on the right page to find your mission in life. You are important! The world needs desperately your kind of goodness and strength of character. Your mission can leave this legacy: "He is such a caring and wonderful person—I want to be like that." Your positive self-image is the first step that will launch you to success in your life's mission.

How do you find your life's high and honorable mission? Begin by *asking some basic questions:*

What would I do if I knew I could not fail?

What would I really like to do with the one and only life I have to live?

What cause could I connect with that I'd be willing to die for?

Some people know their mission early in life, early enough to plan ahead, get the necessary grades, save enough money, and attend the right school. Others discover it later in life, perhaps as a second career in retirement, after their financial needs have been met. Yet others stumble upon the calling for their lives in the most inopportune moments. Such was the case for one young man living in Israel.

Bill Rhodes married at the age of 26 and his wife was expecting their first child when he studied ancient Semitic languages and archaeology and completed his master's degree from Jerusalem University college in Jerusalem.

A devout Christian, Bill would spend quiet time each morning in prayer, seeking God's quiet communication and wisdom. His wife, Laura, recalls that to find complete solitude Bill would literally follow the words of Jesus: "Go away by yourself, in a closet, to pray" (Matthew 5:6). Alone on a hill overlooking Jerusalem, Bill committed his life to whatever calling God gave him.

The answer, which he believes came from God, at first seemed incomprehensible. It didn't make sense, it couldn't be right. But the idea wouldn't go away. It fastened to a desire, and then the desire became stronger. The vision and the dream started to come together clearly in his mind. He embraced his calling with conviction—to become a medical missionary in Africa, bringing hope for tomorrow to thousands of persons.

The only problem was that Bill's course of studies had led him down a completely different path. He had to start all over again—and he was married with two children! However, with his wife's support, encouragement, and willingness to support the family, Bill pursued studies to earn a bachelor of science degree. Doors opened to him to help support his family. Laura not only worked but home-schooled their children while Bill was a full-time student in medical school and then while he was completing his residency.

Seventeen years later Bill and Laura and their children, who now numbered four, packed up what little they had accumulated during their twenty-three years of marriage and under the auspices of Africa Inland Mission moved to Kapsowar, Kenya. Together with his family, Bill learned the Kiswahili language and became Kapsowar Hospital's only surgeon, performing every kind of surgery possible for the local people. He has delivered babies and performed brain surgery, serving as the area's only physician. He even takes care of the many AIDS patients in that region, often risking his own life for his mission.

Life's not worth living until you are committed to someone or something you'd be willing to die for. Would you sacrifice your life for your career or profession? I have often said I would if such a sacrifice were necessary for my mission.

Begin by examining your value system. Would you die for things? Toys? Treasures? I don't think so. Would you give up your life for people? For your spouse? For your child? I think you would. Now your life's mission is becoming clear.

Next, *examine your natural gifts and talents*. Every person has inherited gifts waiting to be discovered and developed. Every individual is a universe made up of a mix of DNA that has never before come together out of a mother's womb. Born into a negative environment, your gifts must be shielded and sheltered from the negative forces that could silence the golden cry in your subconscious: "See me, set me free to become fulfilled in a divine mission." Saint Paul offered these words to his young friend Timothy, making a life-affirming challenge: "Neglect not the gift that is in you" (1 Timothy 4:14). Don't throw away tomorrow!

So why do millions of humans go from birth to death never connecting with the spark of the divine image within themselves? One reason people throw away their tomorrows is that negative forces pollute their mental system. Then the positive forces that could detoxify this negative mental atmosphere are unrecognized or simply untapped.

Also, the process of defining your mission is just that—a process. For myself, the process was simple and specific. At the age of five years, I met my Uncle Henry, a Princeton-educated missionary who was returning from China for the first time. He ruffled my hair and said enthusiastically,

"Robert, you're going to be a minister when you grow up!" I heard it. I felt it. I accepted the vision. I embraced it with head and heart. I never for a moment lost sight of that mission. I have lived in and for tomorrow ever since. I still do!

But most people find that their mission evolves more gradually. Career changes occur, people come and go, and unforeseen possibilities present themselves. Positive pressures arise that call for midflight corrections in the vision that has been compelling and controlling their mission.

Not long ago I interviewed Dr. Steven Sample on my weekly television program, *The Hour of Power*. Dr. Sample's impressive résumé reveals how his mission evolved. In 1991 he became the president of the University of Southern California. During his tenure there, USC has emerged as a world leader in the fields of communications and multimedia technologies and has solidified its status as one of the world's leading research universities. In 1998 Dr. Sample was elected to the prestigious National Academy of Engineering for his contributions to consumer electronics and leadership in interdisciplinary research and education. He was then elected chairman of the Association of American Universities, a group consisting of sixty-two major research universities, both public and private, in the United States and Canada. He has also served as co-founder and chairman of the Association of Pacific Rim Universities, consisting of thirty-four major research universities from Russia to New Zealand.

I share the details of his credentials because, as you read his advice and wisdom, you might think that you were listening to a theologian. His perspective and wisdom are not heard enough in the secular centers of higher education.

"I was born and raised in a suburb of St. Louis, Missouri, then moved when I was six to a farm in St. Charles County," Dr. Sample told us. "As a young man I was a professional musician playing timpani with the St. Louis Philharmonic. I also played in various dance bands and smoky cabarets in St. Louis County. But then I decided to become an engineer. Eventually, after I earned my doctorate, I became a professor of engineering. Later, I went into administration, as so many of us do in academia."

Dr. Sample's wide and varied experiences as a musician, an engineer, a scholar, and a leader have given him the opportunity to share his wisdom with thousands of young people. During our interview he shared a portion of an amazing commencement address he gave at the University of Nebraska. At this secular university, he asked the graduates three questions.

"The first question you as graduates need to think about is: How do you really feel about money? The second question: How do you really feel about children and your obligation to children? And third: How do you feel about God? My experience over the years has taught me that if you can confront these three questions early in your adulthood and find answers that work for you (not my answers or anyone else's, but *your* answers), you will be a much happier and more productive person throughout your life."

Dr. Sample then shared the personal advice he received as a young man from a former General Motors executive:

"I had just earned tenure as a young faculty member at Purdue University when I was offered a very lucrative industrial position. The executive said to me, 'Steve, what you and your wife have to figure out is how you really feel about money.' He continued: 'I'm not saying that you should feel one way or the other, but so many people in this world never figure it out for themselves. There are many people pursuing money who might be happier in a more altruistic profession.' And then he said, 'There are also many people in altruistic professions—teaching, the ministry, and so on—who would be happier pursuing money.' He concluded, 'If you can get the answer right for yourself, you'll be able to address many of life's choices in a more definitive and satisfying way.'

"So my wife and I thought about it, and we decided money wasn't all that important to us. We would stay with academic work. And we've been very happy with that decision."

Then Dr. Sample asked the graduates how they felt about children. "The second question I ask you is so important in the United States today because our society, like it or not—and we hate to admit it—treats children worse than almost any other industrialized nation in the world. This is a very tough place for children, with weak family structures, high levels of violence, poor-quality health care for many children, and some of the worst schools in the world. So the question I pose to you students is: How do you feel about children? And what do you think your obligations are to children? What commitments are you willing to make to your own children, or to the children of other people?"

Dr. Sample then explained his belief in the value of long-term, stable marriages. "My wife and I have been married for over four decades. We came to our marriage with a strong commitment to making it work. Both of us were willing to go more than halfway. My parents had gone through a very difficult divorce just prior to our being married, and that was unquestionably the most painful thing that ever happened to me. We were determined to give our children and our grandchildren the gift of a stable home life.

"The third question I asked the graduating students was: How do you feel about God? I think this is a more embarrassing question for many people than how they feel about sex. By asking this question, I'm not trying to sell you a set of religious beliefs. The question is not how *should* you feel about God, but how *do* you feel about God.

"It's all right with me if you believe there is no God, or that there is a God but you don't wish to have a relationship with him. But I have found that the majority of people duck this question altogether. It is too scary for them to seriously address.

"Millions of people in this country regularly attend religious services, yet haven't any idea how they feel about God. And there are millions of agnostics who feel that questions pertaining to God are unanswerable or unimportant, but who can't fully suppress their concerns for the spiritual aspects of their own existence.

"But one of the deepest and most abiding concerns, in all places and for all peoples, is our feeling for and relationship with God.

"My point is that you may be able to run from your true feelings about God or non-God, but it is difficult to hide from them in the long term. Thus it is to your advantage to confront these feelings sooner rather than later."

Dr. Sample, a scientist, an electrical engineer, and one of the most esteemed men in the academic world, then shared how he personally confronted what he believes about God. He had been a nominal Episcopalian for thirty-five years—a "cultural Christian." And then, quite by accident, he came into serious contact with the Bible. That began a new chapter in his life.

"I had taken a job temporarily in Chicago, and living in a suburb, each day I took a commuter train into the city. I had time to read, so I thought as a matter of cultural education I should read the Bible. I soon learned that if you ride a commuter train with a Bible in your hand, no one wants to sit by you. That was a little side benefit. Anyway, as I was reading the Bible I tried to understand why that text has made such a huge impact on our society and indeed around the world.

"Ultimately I read all of the Bible, but it was the four Gospels that really had an effect on me. It wasn't a flash of lightning; it wasn't an epiphany in that sense. But by reading the Gospels several times, I began to see that there was something here that went far beyond cultural Christianity. I found myself praying a personal prayer to God and to Jesus Christ several times a day. From that time on it has been a very important part of my life."

Dr. Sample concluded: "The central business of a university is the education of its students—undergraduates, graduate students, postdoctoral students, professional students—but the focus is on the development of individuals through the cultivation and enrichment of the human mind and spirit. My religious faith has helped keep me focused on the core values of the university, which are human values, people values."

Wow—what a mission Dr. Sample has: to help educate the next generation about values and to nourish them intelluctually. And it came from examining his values, discovering his natural gifts—and beginning the process.

To find a mission that gives purpose and meaning to your own life, *let your mission be bigger than who you are—make your goals big enough for God to fit in. Then you will find a mission that truly gives purpose and meaning to life.*

Recently I came across another story of a man who had quite a different approach to finding the special mission God had for him. I found it in a piece called "Finding Himself on an Island," written by Lori Basheda and published in the *Orange County Register* on October 11, 2003.

So you're having a midlife crisis, wrestling with questions like where are you going and what's the point?

Do like Sean Downs did, and get a second life. One that includes tribal villagers. On a primitive island. In Indonesia.

Sean Downs lives in Laguna Hills. He has a supportive wife and two charming children. And a

Hearst-castle-worthy pool in the backyard of his well-appointed home. He is in charge of a 300-person Irvine division of Fair Isaac, a software company traded on the New York Stock Exchange.

But at forty, some serious questions began knocking around inside his head. "What responsibility do I have to a higher purpose when I've been so blessed?" And "What should I do with the second half of my life?"

Downs read the midlife "catalyst" book *Half Time*. And he was energized by the theme of moving from "success to significance."

He took a three-month sabbatical from work. And he set out to find—the perfect wave. Well, there's no law that says you can't ponder significance and surf at the same time. Besides, he was burned out. He needed to think.

And it was the waves that drew Downs to his destiny.

First he and his family flew to Bali, where he had surfed before. But this time the waters were too crowded. Downs's wife, Kathryn, and children, Avery, thirteen, and Brian, nine, returned to Laguna Hills. He took a prop plane to the island of Sumba. There, word had it, he would find a quiet resort on a killer surf break.

That wasn't all he found.

Sumba (pronounced "Soom-bah") is one of the poorest islands in the Indonesian archipelago. Nearly 40 percent of children died by age eight from dysentery or other disease because there was no clean water. Most of the inhabitants on the west side lived in huts made of grass and bamboo. There was no electricity.

The island had gained a note of fame on the Discovery Channel for its megalithic gravesites and tribal rituals but was largely forgotten when it came to aid.

This is apparent just a few hundred yards from Nihiwatu, a resort opened by Claude Graves of New Jersey in 2001. It employs only islanders.

Graves told Downs it was his mission to pull the Sumba people from poverty by creating jobs for them. His dream: to start a foundation to improve the lives of the Sumbanese. Downs knew this was the moment he had been waiting for.

"I was scared at first," he remembers. "Is this a foolish venture to commit my money to, my time?"

He returned to Laguna Hills three weeks later and presented his wife with the plan. "I just took this step of faith," he says. Kathryn pledged her support. "This isn't a flash in the pan," she says. "It's a lifelong commitment."

A Costa Mesa attorney helped him incorporate the nonprofit Sumba Foundation, dedicated to improving health and education on the island without disrupting traditions.

That was April 2002. The foundation's first project was to buy a drilling rig in Indonesia and ship it by ferry to the island along with a crew to train the locals to use it. In eighteen months, six wells were drilled, bringing clean water to 1,500 people.

In April the foundation employed the villagers to build a medical clinic and airlifted $150,000 worth of vitamins, antibiotics, and malaria medication donated from the Santa Barbara charity Direct Relief.

And in May a team of eight Surfers Medical Association doctors arrived in Sumba to volunteer their services, treating hundreds of villagers the first day.

Downs then traveled to Sumba to begin a malaria eradication program, distributing sleeping nets and medicine. Each trip reinforces for him that he is doing the right thing.

Downs saw that village schools had holes in the roofs and floors. Broken scraps of furniture served as desks. The children had no pencils or paper. They drew with sticks in the sand. Most students dropped out by sixth grade.

The foundation has sponsored three schools so far, building desks and bathrooms that they never had before and donating pencils and paper and soccer balls.

At one village, Downs and his brother and two friends produced a Frisbee and began tossing it to each other. Crowds quickly gathered. People came out of the hills to watch this flying disc. Soon they were chanting, "Woooo-woop, woooowoop," with each toss. The Americans gave the Frisbee to the tribal chief. He tossed it, hitting someone in the crowd in the chest. "They thought it was the funniest thing they had ever seen." The game went on for hours. When Downs returned to the village a few months later, he asked what happened to the Frisbee. "Apparently they played with it until it just disintegrated."

Downs declines to reveal how much money his family has given to the foundation. "The only criteria was that it had to be an amount that was significant to us," he says.

Graves donates a portion of the money he makes at his resort. But Downs says private donations make up the chief income. He collected nearly $100,000 this year from business associates, church friends, surf friends. A Newport Beach doctor heard about the foundation, flew to Sumba, and then wrote a $5,000 check. A Mission Hospital doctor recently donated $10,000.

After Downs shared his Sumba story at his church recently, four Orange County families asked if they could adopt a village. They are paying for a well to be dug, school repairs, and mosquito nets. The families, their thirteen children included, will travel to Sumba in July to meet the people they're helping.

"I was just trying to find my purpose in life," Downs says. "I had no idea."

Sean Downs went on a vacation—and found a fabulous tomorrow.

∾

FOUR

Choose Positive Values That Empower Your Future

Your values will shape your destiny.

"Johnny," the grateful mother said to her son, "you were so helpful to me today that I'm giving you a special thank-you." She reached out her open palm to offer him a quarter. "Johnny, you can go to the store and buy anything you please. Have fun shopping."

The boy was ecstatic. This was back many years ago when twenty-five cents could go a long way toward satisfying a child's imagination. In the store Johnny was attracted to balloons. Tempted, he looked at the choice of sizes and colors, but he laid them down and moved on. A box of crayons! Yes! No. Tiny cars! Yellow? Blue? Red? "I don't know," he said to himself. A kite? Then, finally . . . whistles. Yes! Yes! He made his selection. Then he headed for the register, excited by his purchase with his one and only coin. The shopkeeper applauded his choice, took his money, handed him his brand-new whistle, and watched him run out of the store. Just outside, he put the whistle to his lips and blew. It was loud. It was beautiful. He made music all the way home! He had always wanted a whistle, and now he had one! But even before he reached home his satisfaction had run its course. Bored with his new toy, he threw it on the grass. Then, frustrated and unfulfilled, in tears he cried out to himself, "A whistle! Why did I waste my quarter on a whistle? I didn't want a whistle after all."

Shakespeare wrote in *The Merchant of Venice,* "You shall seek all day ere you find them; and when you have them, they are not worth the search."

In our compulsive quest for satisfaction, we have become a throwaway society. We throw away food, throw away clothes, throw away appliances. Last year's cell phone, computers, VCRs are all obsolete. Technology is a throwaway industry. The result? Our trash containers are overflowing, and community landfills have become mountains as tons of throwaways are added daily. All the while, TV sitcoms, tabloids, and movies bombard us with throwaway relationships, throwaway marriages, throwaway families, yes, even throwaway lives.

No wonder we are in danger of throwing away time-tested values, classical music, classical sexual morality, and classic Judaic-Christian values. Careless, cavalier, and uncommitted, we too often throw away these classic values by accepting what is, at least for today, fashionable.

Not a few people throw away their tomorrows because their value system is confused and conflicted and they are driven more by primitive, uncivilized passions than by civilized values. Money, ego, sex, pleasure, power, and control are all powerful and primeval passions within the human personality. Passions are the expression of natural emotional or biological hungers in the human being. They are natural inner drives in human personality that can and will shape our behavior for better or worse.

Passions are not necessarily negative expressions of human beings, but they can compete with or divert human resources such as time and energy from values that build character and ultimately fulfill life with a satisfying pride and self-respect. Passion and human desires are often in conflict with values. I love to be slender and attractive and physically fit in body. That's a value! But I love to eat. That's a passion!

Values must transcend primitive biological desires and bring civility to primeval emotional outbursts. Values, not instinctive desires, must define and design our morality. Values will determine how passions and desires are disciplined to promote character development. Passions are innate emotions distinguished from reason, but values are chosen. Values are the moral, ethical, and spiritual principles that guide, control, direct, manage, release, or restrain our passionate energy.

All passions are powerfully important, and all passions will be shaped, one way or another, by values. The values you choose will design the architecture of your personality, shaping it toward positive or negative ends. Wholesome values create joy and enthusiasm, which generate energy. But when the architecture of your personality is dominated by negative values, your moods may be morose, melancholy, morbid, or even mean. When primitive passions are left unmanaged by honorable human values, the creature that evolves will be virtually uncivilized. Civility is dangerously vulnerable.

What really matters most in your life?

What motivates you?

Are you passion driven?

Are you purpose driven?

For the past fifty years, I have lived in southern California, a place with a crazy mix of ideologies, politics, and religions. The culture here is "Anything goes!"—in pleasure or money pursuits, in relationships, in marriage or sex. Freedom in this community verges on cultural anarchy. And through its entertainment industry and its trendsetting power, California is the leading edge for cultural changes all over the world. The modern world of "anything goes," a world without a solid grounding in values, is a world without purpose or direction. In such a world, we need a renaissance of positive values.

I was once asked by a reporter from a famous and successful erotic magazine, "Dr. Schuller, is there any passion humans can experience that gives as much or more pleasure than sex?" My answer was "yes." It is a happy tear in the eye at a wedding or a celebration, at a graduation or an award ceremony, at the playing of a national anthem or a spiritual festival, or at a funeral when warm memories of care and compassion fill the heart with an indescribable love.

Yes, it is the happy tears erupting with passionate joy when your heart is moved by a tender, touching, triumphant story in the life of another human being. Or when we sense or see innocence or heroism in a person, such as the Olympian, who exchanges years of ease and pleasure for hard work, training, and sacrifice and earns the gold medal to thunderous applause. Yes, then we are witnessing and experiencing a "God thing." When a true story is told with sincerity to inspire, to uplift, to motivate you to be like the heroes, then your soul is stirred. Hope rises within you and erupts in tears from your eyes. This is spiritual passion, which illuminates the powerful potential of emotional wellness.

The debate over the role of nature versus nurture will probably go on forever, but almost no one believes that we are born with our values absolutely fixed and predetermined. Values are not inherited in genes. Values are chosen from the teachings of parents or teachers, from ideology, philosophy, culture, or religion.

In a doctoral program in education at a prominent university, the professor led students in a discussion on ethics in educational leadership. The discussion was intended to help these future school administrators identify their values.

"What is most important to you?" the instructor asked.

One eager student raised his hand and said, "I think it is honesty. I believe it's important for us to be honest—with our students, our parents, our colleagues."

"Really?" challenged the professor. "What if you had a staff member who was overweight? Would you be honest and tell him that he needed to lose weight?"

"Well . . . ," the grad student stammered. Then he began backpedaling, qualifying when and how he would be honest, grasping for words that would please the professor.

Another student bravely countered, "More than honesty, I believe we need respect for everybody."

"Really?" asked the professor, once again, eyebrows raised. "Even Hitler?"

"Well . . ."

And so it went, with varying suggestions made, revised, qualified. Some suggested that they valued personal responsibility. Finally one suggestion pointed to care and compassion. This value hit a chord with the professor and was apparently what he was waiting to hear.

"The challenge," the professor contended, "is to know what you believe. What do you value? Through what lens do you see your world and those around you? Your values will be shaped by your philosophy."

What was the professor trying to teach these aspiring leaders in education? He was trying to help them identify their own values. After raising their awareness through the introductory discussion, he led them into a lecture on personal philosophy and how it shapes our value systems.

Habitat for Humanity is known around the world for its compassionate caring. Few people know how and why it all began, but I know, for Millard Fuller is my friend.

When Millard Fuller confronted and changed his values, he found real joy and fulfillment.

Millard Fuller was a lawyer and businessman and a millionaire when suddenly his wife left him, but, praise God, he got her back. They both felt that their wealthy lifestyle had driven them away from God and from each other. So they took a big step: "To just give all our stuff away." They did just that, and Habitat for Humanity was born. In Millard Fuller's own words, "Today I consider myself one of the richest people on earth. How can you put a value on what we experience when we dedicate a house for a needy family?"

Millard Fuller's mission was to eliminate poverty housing. He based his mission on the great values from the Bible: "With God all things are possible." "Love your neighbor as yourself." Habitat builds the whole house, including landscaping and all the flowers, and the family is ready to move in.

Millard says, "When you know your neighbor's name, and you try to identify real families with real needs, and you go to them with real love and build houses not *for* them but *with* them, that's loving your neighbor." Habitat houses are not charity. The families have to put in hundreds of sweat-equity hours. And when a house is finished, the family pays for it on the Bible finance plan—no profit, no interest—which makes it affordable to low-income families. Every homeowner for whom Habitat builds is a partner. Each becomes a participant. "It is more blessed to give than to receive." Says Millard, "If you don't allow the recipient to also give, you have left out one of the real important ingredients of the Christian faith that we profess." That's Millard's philosophy for the success of Habitat for Humanity.

Habitat for Humanity will build their 200,000th house this year, which will house 1,000,000 people. The organization believes that everybody who is made in the image of God should have a decent place to live on terms they can afford to pay. All of this is done through mostly volunteer labor. Local Habitat for Humanity organizations, called affiliates, receive applications from families who are homeless or living in inadequate housing and whose income does not qualify them for a loan from a bank or a savings and loan association.

"Obviously, we can't wave a magic wand and build a house for everybody who needs one immediately. It's like a little mustard seed of faith: you build one, and you get a little stronger, and you build another one, you get a little stronger, and you build two more. But," Millard Fuller says, "we always keep the goal in mind of building a house for everybody because the God we serve is the God of us all. The God we serve is a God of a hundred sheep. We know that God is also the God of the lost sheep. There may be ninety-nine in the fold, but if there is one still outside, spiritually, economically, psychologically, that's one too many." So Millard Fuller keeps on building homes through Habitat for Humanity.

On September 9, 1996, at a ceremony in the White House, Millard Fuller, the founder of Habitat for Humanity, received the Presidential Medal of Freedom, the nation's highest civilian honor, for the important contributions he is making not only to our nation, but also to communities in more than fifty countries around the world. Today, Habitat for Humanity is at work in one hundred countries.

Your worth as a human being will be measured by the quality of the values that you choose.

In college, our psychology professor made us memorize these lines:

Sow an idea—reap an act.
Sow an act— reap a habit.
Sow a habit—reap a character.
Sow a character—reap a destiny.

Every human being—intuitively, accidentally, or intentionally—evolves into a "character."

Character is the definition of your personhood. It is the essential core that defines and describes your reputation. Character is conceived and born in the arena where your life's principles are chosen. Then character will shape your choices and decisions. And character will be the force in your personality that will motivate you to set goals and manage your life to meet them. And strong character will survive any outcome. Ralph Waldo Emerson said, "Character is that which we can do without success." What you are is more important that what you do.

There are, in the final analysis, no great or nongreat people. We are all the same. The difference is that some people are committed to noble and honorable values. Great values deliver great character.

I have become friends with many highly esteemed people in my lifetime. All are molded not by uncontrolled passion but by what I call value-controlled passion. This drives them to unselfish greatness.

Mother Teresa was recently beatified in the Roman Catholic Church. She kept many a person from throwing away their tomorrows. She was, in her own words, a human in whose heart Jesus Christ lived. Her mission: "To do something beautiful for God." Her strategy can be found in a handwritten blessing to me: "To Dr. Schuller—Be all and only for Jesus, let Him use you without consulting you first."

Two of my greatest honors were to be invited to her funeral in Calcutta, India, and then to her beatification ceremony at the Vatican in Rome. Compassion was, in my judgment, the dominant value that drove her. It was this spiritual value that impassioned her to bring love and hope into the tomorrows of thousands of suffering people.

• • •

When and where can we be inspired to choose high and honorable values?

Nature sets some values. Many must be viewed as nonnegotiable. All life on planet earth requires clean air and clean water. Nature cannot take care of itself. Human beings must preserve an environment in which birds sing and flowers bloom. If we disregard these values long enough, our planet will die.

Traditions deliver deep values. Consider— respectfully and courageously—the power of tradition in shaping our values. Governance in primitive culture was often controlled—for good or ill—by tribal tradition.

In the awe-inspiring musical *Fiddler on the Roof,* Tevye, the head of his family living in the small village of Anatevka, struggles with traditions and values. In Anatevka, he says, there were traditions for everything—how to eat, how to sleep, how to wear clothes. For instance, they always kept their heads covered and always wore a little prayer shawl, to show their constant devotion to God. Because of their traditions, everyone knew who they were and what God expected them to do.

Tevye is molded by tradition, but he has the capacity to compromise until his last daughter asks his approval to marry an atheist. This he cannot compromise and loudly declares, ". . . some things I will not, cannot allow—tradition!" Yet people abandon proven traditions. Why? Sometimes it is a result of youthful rebellion. Other times it is wanting to catch a new wave attracting attention, to feed the ego. Revisionism attracts attention when unknown authors find their shocking theories published in journals, columns, op-ed pieces, and books. Even responsible publishers can fall prey to this seduction. And the Internet will publish anything.

When you throw away yesterday, you also throw away a part of tomorrow. If you forget where you came from, you will not long remain where you are, which is why I keep my framed infant baptismal dress hanging on my study wall.

Tradition in culture is like the root system of a plant. The root system must be preserved from toxic invasion. Neglect the root system, and the fruit tree will secretly begin to die.

Tradition is the great protector of proven historic values; it preserves life-forms from negative deviation or extinction. Rene Du Bois, father of sociobiology, discovered that if you change the sociology of a life-form, you change the living organism. Most often it will die—or allow its nature to be altered in its struggle to survive. Change the natural habitat of the human being, and you change the character. Take Adam out of the Garden and put him in freeway traffic with horns, sirens, and fumes, and he loses his spiritual awareness.

But tradition can be—and often has been—the first and foremost obstacle to progress. It has aborted many tomorrows that would have helped society become healthy and prosperous. "If it works, don't fix it," the traditionalist warns. But the positive thinker strives to be creative. "If it works, improve it," the creative mind declares. Certainly, misapplied tradition can be oppressive and restrictive of progress, but there is equally great danger in reacting against a tradition simply because it is old and out of fashion. "Be not the first to lay the old aside— nor yet the last by which the new is tried." Be assured that most traditions must have had some wisdom and real value or they never would have survived long enough to become a recognized and respected tradition. Rejecting a tradition and replacing it with a vacuum allows untried and untested avant-garde values to move in. Wisdom declares that setting aside traditional values is a serious business, not be undertaken lightly. "Before we take down fences, we should learn why they were put up in the first place."

Religion is the power of positive spiritual passions. No other institution matches the power of religions institutions to mold human personalities with traditional human values. Certainly the religious faith taught to me as a child has been the primary source of my value system. I was brought up on the Ten Commandments and the Sermon on the Mount. From this Judaic-Christian foundation I received a strong set of values imbued with faith, hope, and love. This faith has delivered energy and enthusiasm into my life. These values motivated me to say "yes" to great ideas, to maintain an "I will not quit" attitude, and to have the courage to say "no" to the alluring values that come from a dehumanizing, secular culture.

In 1967 I attended the World Psychiatric Congress in Madrid, Spain, along with over four thousand psychiatrists from around the world. The final plenary session carried the theme "Human Values in Psychiatry." Three distinguished psychiatrists each submitted a value, and when the first lecturer spoke on "Faith," I was shocked. "Never knock it; look for it in your patients," he said. "Build on it. It is an expression of positive mental activity that is a potential power force in human personality." The second doctor spoke on "Hope": "An awesome, powerful human value," he declared. The third psychiatrist spoke on "Love": "The most powerful of all human values," he told us. These three human values, the world of mental and emotional healing professionals were told, are the ultimate positive values.

Where did these psychiatrists find these power values? All three were men raised in cultures in which the Judaic-Christian religion dominated and the Holy Bible was respected. In this book, we read how the followers of Jesus Christ were taught by Paul, "And now abide faith, hope, and love, and the greatest of these is love" (1 Corinthians 13:13).

Positive spiritual passion is the power source of human values that transform people from selfish, greedy, arrogant, and duplicitous creatures into beautiful human beings who are unselfish, generous, caring, and compassionate.

Choose your values carefully. Seek and accept the spiritual faith that boosts and blesses those values that will shape you into a more beautiful human being.

From the traditions of Judaic-Christian culture come two more all-important human values—humility and honesty. All of the great people I've known in my life show a bold and brave commitment to these twin virtues. Honesty will be the fallout of humility. And humility will be the fallout of honesty. If you are humble, you'll dare to say, "I need help, I can't do it alone." If you are honest, you'll be free to accept the help you need: "Thank you! I needed that." Say it even if you have to share the credit. Remember, "God can do great things through the person who doesn't care who gets the credit."

Honesty and humility will draw support to your side. "You can trust him" will be the word about you. "You can believe in her" will be the reputation spread about you by those who deal with you. Live to earn respect and trust from those around you. Humility and honesty will deliver that!

My father-in-law, Lou DeHaan, was a simple Iowa farmer. One day his nephew came to call with a specific agenda. "Uncle Lou," he said to my father-in-law, "I'm going to start a new restaurant in Sioux City." That was the biggest city in northwest Iowa. "I need capital. Do you have cash to invest in my new business?" Uncle Lou was intimidated. He paused. He hedged. "Don't worry, Uncle Lou, you'll get your money back. You can trust me. And you can set the interest rate." So Dad gave his nephew what he asked for, which was almost all of his modest retirement nest egg. The deal was done. Handshake only. No paper. Just promises. And no interest. One year later the restaurant went bankrupt. The settlement left nothing to be given to the creditors. Dad lost every penny. His nephew, embarrassed, moved to another state. He couldn't face his Uncle Lou, who had lost his entire investment.

Years later, when Dad was not too many years from retirement, he got a letter in the mail. Enclosed was a small check from his nephew. The next month, another check. And in the next twenty-four months, the checks came until they added up to repayment in full of the loan Dad had made to his nephew. Bankruptcy had legally wiped out the debt, but Dad's nephew lived by values higher and nobler than the law.

Then, as Christmas was approaching, a big truck pulled up to Dad's yard. Off the truck came a large box. The driver put it on the front porch. "What's this?" my mother-in-law asked.

"I have no idea," Dad answered.

They opened it, and the first thing they saw was an envelope—from Dad's nephew. Inside was not money—he was now all paid up—but a note: "You never charged me interest, Uncle Lou. So I'm sending you a special thank-you gift." Underneath the wrapping paper was a large and luxurious, upholstered La-Z-Boy wingback recliner.

Yes, values shape character, and character shapes the person.

But what happens when values clash? When you are equally committed to values that unexpectedly are in conflict? Work it out. Face conflict with resolution therapy. Just don't throw away tomorrow.

Often the conflict is not between good and bad but rather between good and good. Or between good and better. Or between good and best. Or between mediocrity and excellence.

Conflict can arise between building a growing business and

building a great marriage with time for the children. Or perhaps you are torn between paying to send your child to a fine private school and paying to provide better care for your elderly mother.

How do you make a decision when competition between your chosen values requires that you choose one over another?

Consider justice versus mercy. In America and most of the developed world, people are free to choose their philosophy and their faith. But the choices are not all the same. "An eye for an eye" was the doctrine prior to Jesus. Vengeance was accepted as an expression of justice, which in more than one culture and religion has meant bloody wars to "get even" and to "fight injustice" with the sword. Then Jesus came teaching nonjudgmental love. Forgiveness became the premier value. "Justice and mercy must embrace each other," and many Christians believe that happened when Christ died on the cross. Christians are taught that when a choice must be made between justice and mercy, let it be on the side of mercy.

Or consider the predicament of surviving. Survival is the primal human value. When we are in harm's way and our lives are threatened by an armed enemy or by a terminal disease, all other values pale in comparison with the value of saving our lives.

Defense of family and faith should be an important value in everyone's life. When spouse or children come under unfair attack, suddenly our priorities shift, and we spend the time and money and energy that it takes to support the value of family.

Recovery after physical or financial reversals may suddenly become a value of highest significance. Call this "damage control." Retirement was a top value until the market collapse of 2002 wiped out the stock of many retired people. For some, recovery meant going back to work.

Our daughter Carol lost her leg in a tragic accident. When she was in high school, she was introduced to handicap skiing and was given an opportunity to make the U.S. Disabled Ski Team. Good values conflicted: stay with school, or leave home to go all out for the sport that could put her on her own? We saw her need to develop a strong "I can do it" character in those early teenage years as all-important, so we did not block her leaving high school before she had earned her diploma. She chose to continue her education through correspondence courses. Was it the right decision? She did go on to set records on the ski slopes, clocked at 70 mph on one ski. This developed a superstrong "I can do it" character and self-confidence, which has led to a super success as an adult.

What about ambition, the drive to advance professionally, academically, or financially? As Robert Browning said, "A man's reach should exceed his grasp, or what's heaven for?" But, you may ask, isn't ambition dangerous? It can be, unless you have an ethical, moral, spiritual, and human values system that immunizes you against dishonesty, duplicity, selfishness, greed, or crude and cruel competition.

What about contentment? Should this not be a high and holy value? The apostle Paul extolled this value in these words: "I have been honored, I have been dishonored. I have acquired wealth, I have lost money. I have had good health and I have had problems—I've lived! And I have learned in whatever state I find myself therewith to be content" (Philippians 4:11–12).

What about happiness? Does money buy happiness? My dear friend psychology professor Martin Seligman of the University of Pennsylvania and Ed Diener of the University of Illinois, Urbana-Champaign, did an ambitious analysis of more than 150 studies on wealth and happiness. The analysis showed, "Extra money doesn't buy much extra happiness. That happiness comes from social relationships, enjoyable work . . . a sense of meaning." Bottom line: "Money may not buy happiness, but happiness might buy money" (reported by Sharon Begley, *Wall Street Journal,* Aug. 13, 2004).

You may need to reprioritize or revise your scale of values as you move through the stages of life. This may not be easy. In fact, it can be very painful. Are you six years old and in first grade? Or are you an adolescent? These phases of life could not be more different. Are you in your early twenties? In your thirties? In your forties, facing a midlife crisis? In your sixties, looking at retirement? Are your children gone and scattered? Are you in your seventies, with your body changing and your friends passing on? Is the light at the end of the tunnel eternal light?

A friend of ours recently gave up her Rolls Royce and her 10,000-square-foot mansion to move into a tri-level retirement home where she'll live in a 1,200-square-foot apartment. She suffered a slight stroke and can no longer manage a grand lifestyle. If she suffers further damage to her health, she can move into the health-care wing of her new home, where she will have medical care available around the clock. Life dictates change, and our priorities must change as well.

The wisdom of Ecclesiastes 3 tells us:

To everything there is a season.
A time for every purpose under heaven.
A time to be born,
And a time to die;
A time to plant,
And a time to pluck
what is planted.

How would your values and priorities change if you were told you had only seven days to live? In a recent interview, Mrs. Schuller was surprised by this question. She has been a believer and follower of Jesus Christ all her life, and her faith has shaped and sustained her from a little girl to the grandmother she is today.

Smiling broadly, with glowing eyes, she spoke words that echoed throughout the studio. "Well, I'd make no changes. I'm so happy with the life I've lived. As my husband always says, 'So live that when you come to the end of your life you'll have pride behind you, love around you, and hope ahead of you.'" Smiling the smile of contentment, she added, "There are no regrets, so I would spend the last seven days of my life saying 'thank you ... thank you ... thank you' to friends, family, and most of all to Jesus Christ."

How do you choose your life values? When the values offered to you in society are confusing and conflicting and riddled with passions, how do you choose? Use both your head and your heart.

Start with your head. Be intelligent. Understand that the basic "emotional atom" from which a happy character is built is self-respect, self-esteem, humble pride. I contend that the most deplorable and destructive emotion is shame—humiliation, dishonor, and disgrace, the exact opposite of pride. No ultimate value surpasses self-respect, or self-esteem. So choose values that build healthy self-esteem in yourself and all other human beings.

Within this paradigm, prepare to appraise the many contradictory values available to you today in the uncommitted culture around you. Ask these questions:

1. Will the values I choose really help people? Someone wisely said, "The greatest need is the need to be needed." The secret of success is to find a need and fill it. Will this philosophy inspire me and others to choose values of altruism, generosity, and self-sacrifice?

2. If I choose to live with these values, will I bring humble and honest honor to my family, my friends, my community, and, of course, to my reputation?

3. Will the people I care about the most respect me for who I have become and what I have done? And will others whom I respect be attracted to me and enjoy being my friend?

4. Will these values increase my hope and happiness for tomorrow and my tomorrows to come?

I was raised in a farming community made up of stalwart Dutch immigrants. We were all Protestant Christians with a strong belief in God and in the Bible. The values of that community were strong and clear. I embraced those transparent values, and they led me to a very fulfilling life. In that culture and that Bible, I found *"God-lines"* that became my *guidelines*.

It is crystal clear to me today that those values were—and always will be—timeless, classical, not changing with the fashions or the times.

How have they served me? That question is best answered from this perspective, two years shy of my eightieth birthday.

In my entire life, my calling to be a minister of religion was challenged only once—when I entered the psychology classroom in Hope College. I wanted to be a preacher because I was called to help human beings become creative, constructive, happy, healthy persons. That was the life I was enjoying, so I had to share it. Like when you hear some exciting music, read a great book, or see a gorgeous view, you want to run to your special friend and enthusiastically unload, "Come here! Read this! Listen to this!" My happy, healthy life came from the positive values inherent in my positive religious faith.

Enter psychology. I began to question my chosen career of being a preacher. Perhaps I could reach more people as a secular psychologist than as a preacher wrapped in a religious image that could turn off agnostics, atheists, secularists, or religious sectarians. I might have made that career switch if I had not learned in class one day, "It is unethical for psychologists and psychiatrists to impose their value system on their patients or clients." That really disturbed me—even though I could see and appreciate the ethical wisdom of that professional policy. "But what if the emotional and mental condition I'm supposed to treat has its sick roots in a patient's value system?" I asked. The answers did not satisfy me. My childhood calling was confirmed. "No, don't become a psychologist; become a minister." Religious leaders can become counselors with the freedom to analyze the value systems of troubled people and share the healthiest value system in which emotional wellness can be realized. A clergyperson can counsel the troubled soul to change destructive values with the internal redemptive therapy of a positive faith.

So I stayed with my decision to become a preacher, a pastor. But I would continue in my lifetime to study insights and interpretations in human behavior from the greatest psychiatrists and psychologists in the world. Positive values would be the foundation of my counseling, and the results are fantastic.

I know when I come to the end of my life, I'll have no regrets about the life my values have delivered to me!

I know for sure I'll never say, "Why did I buy that whistle?"

The last word: Make a commitment to nonnegotiable values to motivate you to say yes to life's positive possibilities and to show you how and when to say no to life's negative temptations and distractions. When you have chosen your values, guard them with all your life. Choose the rules and set the boundaries that will protect and project your values. And they will deliver to you a successful and satisfying tomorrow.

∞

FIVE

Let Your Conscience Write Your Rules and Set Your Boundaries

Life without a conscience is a river without banks.

"Good to see you again, Grandpa," Jason, my oldest grandson, said. Jason had just returned from boot camp in the Naval Reserves. The occasion was a family dinner celebrating the birthday of Jason's brother, Chris. We were in the backyard with the aroma of barbecue wafting over us. Then Jason said, "At least here we can talk while we eat."

I was puzzled. "What do you mean, Jason? Certainly you could talk at mealtime at boot camp!"

"Oh, no!" he explained. "The Navy has firm rules, and one rule was complete silence at dinner. No talking."

I laughed and said, "But what if you wanted someone to pass the salt?"

"Oh, we had sign language for everything we needed. For salt we did this. . . ." He held up his index finger. "For pepper, you held up two fingers, and for catsup, we did this." He held up an imaginary catsup bottle, shaking it up and down on his other hand, palm open.

Throughout dinner my grandson regaled us with stories of the Navy's many rules—how they enforce them and why they make them.

His eyes were wide open as he stretched to sit upright, about to make a very important statement. "They have very important rules, and there is a good reason for every rule. They make it loud and clear what the primary rules are."

My friend Nieta Armstrong, a lieutenant colonel in the Marine Corps and a faithful elder in the church, was sent to the Iraq conflict. When she returned home many months later, she gave me a three-by-five plastic card that she said all military personnel were ordered to carry in the pockets of their uniform. The card gave specific rules of engagement for each person representing our country. Nieta pointed out to me how the rules related specifically to treatment of civilians and enemy forces, with the order to respect their dignity at all times.

In every one of life's missions there are rules of engagement. This is true not just in the military but also in the academic, corporate, political, religious, and athletic worlds. Rules drafted, written, approved, communicated, interpreted, and enforced make up most of what is called "governance" in societies—national, regional, and local.

In ancient Rome, as it struggled between republic and empire, Cicero declared, "Liberty without law will lead to anarchy. And liberty will not long be tolerated in an anarchy." That universal principle holds not only in democratic institutions but in our private lives as well.

"How is your new class at school?" I asked my eleven-year-old granddaughter Paige.

"I like it except there are so many rules," she said, scrunching her nose. "School shouldn't have rules. Then it would really be fun, Grandpa."

"But you have rules in your family too," I reminded her. She was silent for a moment.

"But most of those are nice rules, and Daddy and Mom say that we have rules for Julia and me to keep us from getting hurt. So they're really rules of love."

"Yes, but, Paige, do you remember when Governor Schwarzenegger visits us at church? He and Maria share the family rules they have in their home. One rule is that the telephone and television are turned *off* from 4:00 P.M. to 7:00 P.M. This provides 'talk time' for their family, and it also protects their children from seeing lots of stuff on television they shouldn't see."

I recall when psychological libertarians argued that little children and teenagers were being thwarted in the development of their personalities by rules that stifled their natural freedom to be creative. Human freedom should not be restricted, they argued, so long as "no one is hurt."

But this case was lost when a playground for young children was planned without fences.

The play area was fresh and clean with lawn, trees, climbing equipment, and swings. The absence of fences, it was imagined, would be emotionally healthier for the children. "They will not feel oppressed, shut in, or locked in a territory," supporters argued. But what happened when the children finally tested out the playground surprised everyone. The children did not run free and fast from one end of the yard to the other. Without that strong and certain boundary to set safe limits, they had to impose their own limits—by inhibiting themselves. When the border fences were later installed, the children were actually liberated! They ran as fast as they could with open arms until they would fly to a safe stop, sometimes even crashing harmlessly into the chain-link fence on the boundary line.

Then educators were shown a video that further challenged their theories. It showed cars driving across high bridges with no guardrails over deep canyons. Fearful drivers drove their cars in the middle of the bridge! When the guardrails were reinstalled, the drivers felt safe driving closer to the edge. How wrong the assumptions about unrestricted freedom were.

I have lived my life in a century of transition from rules to freedom. When I was a child, our rules were set forth by our religion. Roman Catholics and Protestants alike saw their role as one of rule enforcement. Sermons reminded people of specific rules to curtail questionable private and public behavior. Boundaries were outlined and enforced. Violation of these narrow interpretations of boundaries were labeled "sins," with guilt sure to follow.

Too often the religious rules were narrow, strict, personal interpretations of Biblical laws by religious leaders who formed their own negative opinions from certain Bible verses.

The Main Street USA churches provided platforms to remind you that you were a sinner and admonish you to repent. This gave many religions an oppressive caste, a negative force that many people found too unpleasant to accept.

Then I saw religion enter a major transition as theologians began to remove the fences and the boundaries. Religion, they declared, is meant to liberate, not enslave, so we must do away with all the rules. "The church cannot, must not, dare not, tell you what is or isn't a 'sin,'" leading seminary professors taught upcoming preachers.

Today, religious institutions are downplaying, if not abandoning, their role as conscience molders. No longer are they the primary "rule shapers" for moral and ethical behavior. Even the Bible is no longer universally accepted by all religious leaders as the final word of God. So pilgrims are left without a final authoritative book to be respected as a holy guide to establish rules and boundaries. Confusion reigns as we try to cope with moral and ethical problems more complicated than ever before.

The result? Our ruleless and rootless society is in danger of becoming a ruthless society. That's a tomorrow nobody wants. We need to become a society led by a renewal of a moral and ethical conscience in our leaders, in religion, science, politics, and education. I submit that it is up to individuals and their families to develop a strong private conscience to guide them.

In a world of cultural complexity and confusion, every individual and every institution must cultivate a strong and sensitive conscience to write the rules to be followed in carrying out their mission statement.

My grandson Ethan Milner attended the summer football camp held by his secular high school athletic department. "They really had some strong rules, Grandpa," he told me. "'Respect your own body and respect the bodies of others' was the first rule. 'How do you do this?' the coaches asked. The players answered, 'Say *no* to substance abuse . . . *no* to alcohol, drugs, tobacco, and pornography. Say *yes* to exercise and a healthful diet. Say *yes* to discipline.'"

Yes, you need to decide what kind of a person you want to become. Then you need to decide what kind of rules will set the boundaries and inspire the standards by which you will achieve your moral, ethical, and spiritual goals. The rules must define and describe how your dream contributes to self-respect and pride of personhood for all who are in the dream. Whatever your dream, human dignity must be the highest value. The bottom line of all missions must be: What kind of persons did we shape and create in our enterprise?

But where can you look for the foundation and the formation of a conscience that will put and keep you on the positive path to high ethics and morality?

Surely not in the secular culture, where there are no rules. Where "anything goes," the conscience goes. We find graduate students—premed, law, and other disciplines—cheating on the final exams that will grant them a degree for their chosen career.

In mass communications, we often find the truth buried, forgotten, or twisted through sound bites, certain adjectives, or a sentence taken out of context—ruining reputations and destroying careers and families. Plagiarism in journalism is in danger of becoming a common occurrence, and the Internet runs amok with half-truths and false innuendoes.

There are financial reports of reputable businesses in which the bottom line shows a profit yet the numbers don't exactly add up.

Then there are those having made their mark in the worldly arena: athletes, entertainers, and prominent business people who don't see their special duty to live by ethical rules. Whether he or she is the chairman of the board, the commanding general, or the manager of a donut shop, the final responsibility to uphold the rules falls on their desk, but they choose to ignore it.

There is always the danger that the person at the top may be tempted to foolishly believe that he or she is "above the law." Too many leaders disregard and break the rules in their personal relationships and in their own corporate governance. We see it happen in government, in corporations, in academia, and in religious institutions.

Without high moral rules to guide society, the future is in peril. Don't throw away tomorrow.

What we desperately need is a truly uplifting book and a truly inspiring person to follow. For me, the Bible is the book, and Jesus Christ is the person. That book, and that Lord, help me develop the conscience that can guide me from moment to moment.

Three of the world's major faiths—Judaism, Islam, and Christianity—are all based on the Ten Commandments, which I call "God's Way to the Good Life." My first book was based on these commandments, where I interpreted God's ten rules in positive terms, not as negative, oppressive teachings. The Ten Commandments show that people of all faiths can live together when we are committed to civility, kindness, and compassion.

The Ten Commandments are designed to support our moral architecture. The commandments are not, however, ten separate, free-standing columns, as in an ancient Roman courtyard where, if you knock one column down, the other nine remain standing.

Rather, they are more like the ten major stones of a Roman arch. Each one leans carefully against another, all mutually supporting each other to frame the entrance over a pathway—a pathway that leads to dignity and self-respect. Take out one stone and you risk the collapse of the entire portico. As the Ten Commandments support each other, they in turn protect you.

The seventh commandment, "Thou shalt not commit adultery," is the one most widely talked about in our culture today. It is often ignored, scoffed at, or made fun of, and yet more misery and violence are caused by the breaking of this one commandment than the breaking of any of the other ten. Break this one, and all too readily you break all ten. Lying, stealing, killing, coveting . . . your defense against all of these will fracture.

The seventh commandment is designed to protect you and

me and those we love the most—our families. Determining to play by the rules of your marriage simply makes life easier, more consistent, more harmonious, even more prosperous and pleasurable.

Kobe Bryant's life and career were thrown into turmoil after he was accused of raping a woman. "Guilty or not," as a hairdresser reminded my wife, "he admitted that he did commit adultery!" His conscience, his family, his career, and his reputation suffered horrifically.

Casual sex among young people has gained widespread acceptance in our society, but recently studies from secular universities have shown the negative consequences. Researchers at Harvard conducted a long-term study of married couples who had lived together before getting married and discovered that the "try it out first" approach doesn't work.

Couples who live together before marriage have a much higher rate of divorce and disillusionment in their marriage.

One of my friends is the NBA all-star and three-time World Champion Laker A. C. Green. He recently retired from his winning basketball career, but he still is honored and respected both in the sports world and in society at large. His reputation is spotless, and his faith is a dominant factor in his life. He truly exemplifies the hero status that many young people hold him to, both professionally and personally.

He was inducted into the World Sports Humanitarian Hall of Fame for his A. C. Green Youth Foundation. Founded in 1989, it promotes sexual abstinence among our youth. What a refreshing change!

"The A. C. Green Youth Foundation centers on abstinence and working with individuals who are underprivileged," he told me. "We provide youth basketball camps free of charge for kids from ten to fifteen years old. And we have a curriculum going into the middle schools called Game Plan, which teaches the benefits of abstinence. It's exciting to play a small part."

"Well, it's widely known," I said to A.C., "that you practiced abstinence till marriage."

"Yes," was his reply, "I'm a living example of it. If I can do it in the role that God took me on, traveling throughout the NBA, there's not a teenager that can tell me it's tougher on them."

"That's for sure," I agreed. "Some of the players in basketball have bragged openly about how many affairs they've had."

A.C. nodded his head and continued. "When you have a vision, a purpose, and understand your calling, you can do extraordinary things for God, even in the midst of a peculiar situation. Living in the NBA for twenty years was very peculiar. But at the same time, it did not separate me from the goal I had —the burning passion that God put in my heart: to instill some kind of hope into our future generation, our kids."

Reflecting on his example, I mentioned the studies that show that people who abstain from sexual intercourse until marriage have happier marriages. "They say the reason is that when they make love to their spouse, the spouse doesn't have to compete with other people in their memory systems."

"That's exactly right," A.C. said, his face breaking into a smile. "My wife and I experienced that. We've been married one year, and we can definitely say it's a good thing not to have comparisons in our memories.

"But I meet a lot of kids who have already said yes to sex," he went on to explain. "They have to go through this healing process, which is a forgiving process. It's so much better if you're a virgin when you get married and you have no comparisons."

How today's preteens and teens need the A. C. Green Foundation principles, which are based on the positive faith that is a daily part of A.C.'s life. "Reading the Bible and praying is a daily thing," A.C. said. "You have to have your own individual relationship with Jesus Christ. It can't always be a service on Sunday, because you can't always get there. In my profession, we were playing almost every Sunday. It's every day—a practice or a game. Sometimes you win; sometimes you lose in the goals you have. But in the big goal, you're going to always win."

Thankfully, abstinence before marriage is gaining popularity among our young people. Several of my grandchildren participated in the True Love Waits program at our church and in their local youth groups. In this program, and in others like it, kids learn that there really is no safe and truly satisfying sex before marriage. They learn the dangers, both emotionally and physically, of sex outside the commitment of marriage. They are taught how to stand up and say no to today's secular culture that encourages "safe sex." They come to understand that "true love waits" until that day they are committed before God as "husband and wife till death do us part." Love that waits is true, satisfying, beautiful love. God designed marriage to be the most intimate of all relationships, where husband and wife become one not only physically but emotionally, socially, and spiritually. That's what God had in mind when He created loving sex.

My wife and I have enjoyed well over fifty years of a wonderful, happy, fulfilled marriage by establishing successful rules. Here are some practical rules that have worked so well for us.

1. We have a weekly date night, and nothing in our schedule is allowed to conflict with it. We've done this religiously for our entire marriage, throughout the early years of raising children to now, in our "golden years." We've taken walks as a date, sat and had ice cream or dinner together—whatever it takes just to spend quiet, deliberate time alone as a loving couple.

2. We are each other's best friend, and our most intimate conversations are kept between us and not shared with others. We can be honest and open, knowing that what is said won't go elsewhere.

3. We don't allow ourselves to be put in a compromising situation with a member of the opposite sex.

I made it a rule in my ministry to never take my female secretary or any other female staff member alone out to lunch. Except in an emergency, we will not ride alone with a friend, neighbor, or staff member of the opposite sex. In counseling sessions I do not sit on a sofa next to a woman but behind my desk, facing her. My wife was one of the first women to work behind the scenes in the TV studios in Hollywood. She made it a point to leave the room when conversations became too friendly or too suggestive. She maintained a high level of professionalism and demanded it from others too.

Some people might feel that these rules are too restrictive, that they might cramp their freedom. All I can say is that I never regret having lived by these rules for my life and my marriage. I thank God for them.

Wayne Gretsky, the famous hockey player, and I were guests of Dennis Washington's on his private plane. We were en route from our homes in southern California to the East Coast to a meeting of the Horatio Alger Society Association. We were sponsoring Wayne to be the first Canadian inducted as a member of Horatio Alger.

During the five-hour flight, Wayne and I had a lengthy discussion about our freedom to choose the moral and ethical rules we live by.

Wayne Gretsky made an early and strong commitment to follow the example of Jesus Christ in both his personal and professional lives. This meant he rejected with a positive *no* many amoral, immoral, and unethical practices widely and wildly accepted in the modern secular society. At one point he asked me,

"Dr. Schuller, what do you do and say when you don't approve of someone's lifestyle, but you want to remain friends enough to work with them and not insult or demean them?"

I advised Wayne to open the dialogue with, "I respect you. I like you as a friend. But even as I respect your freedom to choose the rules you decide to follow, I disagree and cannot approve of some of your choices."

Then I applauded Wayne for his outstanding moral lifestyle, "Stay committed to the higher, nobler values that you chose to shape your character. It helps to explain why you are so successful."

A strong moral conscience makes an awesome difference in our personal and professional lives. In short, it creates a psychological environment where emotional wellness evolves.

Now, see the difference a powerful moral conscience makes in our emotional evolution. Moral conscience is not only a voice that says "no." It is also a voice that says, "let's go!"

What is moral conscience? One definition states, "It is a feeling of obligation to do right and be good." That "do right—feel good" feeling promotes emotional well-being in a person.

- Yes, emotional wellness begins with a clear conscience—freedom from guilt. This allows us to live joyously rather than defensively.

- Then with a clear conscience, we dare to believe in ourselves. The power of self-esteem and self-confidence delivers a strong, safe, and satisfying ego.

- Emotional wellness is not possible until we dare to be emotionally open and honest. There is no fear of exposing our true selves and risk being embarrassed by a darker side accidentally revealed, and we are free from the pressures of hypocrisy.

- Then, spontaneous enthusiasm arises in the emotional wellness that is evolving. Only honest and open persons can be genuinely enthusiastic, for there is no fear of Freudian slips that will reveal secret sins.

- Emotionally liberated, we spend our energy in positive spontaneity. We listen. We laugh. We love. We trust goodness when we see it.

- Then, we win friends. Enthusiasm is energy that delivers an appealing personality. Good people are attracted to us and we trust them. Cynicism does not do well in this positive environment. We become enthusiastic communicators and we build happy and healthy relationships. Emotional wellness delivers an exciting life.

- A moral conscience allows us the freedom to conceive and receive creative ideas. Then, out of the blue comes a beautiful dream. Believing in ourselves and in the best people, we become powerful possibility thinkers. The conscience is no longer a voice that says only, "no." It is now a voice that says, "Let's go!"

- Emotional wellness is the reward when we live in the environment of an honorable moral conscience. We are optimistic. We welcome visitors. The sound of the doorbell gives us joy. We are excited when the telephone rings.

- Now we have the courage to welcome God in our life. The word "enthusiasm" is born of the Greek words "en Theos," translated "in God." Emmanuel Kant, one of the greatest philosophers of history, declared that his belief in God was based on two realities: "The starry heavens above and the moral law within." When we live highly moral committed lives we will dare to become believers in a Higher Power. Now we are motivated and we are ready to face the risks and the rewards of tomorrow.

∞

SIX

Measure Tomorrow's Risks and Rewards Carefully

Everything that's nice has its price.

Don't let the fear of taking risks throw away your tomorrow.

Every career has its own occupational hazards. There are many dangers that cannot be prevented even with such safety devices as parachutes, jet releases, hard hats, safety belts, flight jackets, bulletproof vests, shatterproof glass, or vaccination shots. Legal contracts can't always protect you from all anticipated conflicts, and not even insurance can cover all potential losses.

You cannot predict every market change. New competitors can suddenly arise from new research or from mergers. A shortfall in revenues may surprise the CEO, and not even Lloyd's of London will insure "success."

Relationships may be where the hit comes. Partnerships break up. Divorce happens. Key people leave, or even die. Then what? "Prenuptial agreements" can't always safeguard us from all the dangers that may arise when creative teams come apart. There are no protective shields against rebellion, betrayal, disloyalty, or infidelity. Hostile takeovers happen in marriages as well as in companies.

There are those whose life's dream to have a military, police, or firefighting career carries the ultimate risk of giving one's life.

I have had the privilege of meeting many of our nation's great astronauts. For most of them, exploring outer space was a lifelong dream—a passion that consumed them—and risking their life was a price they were willing to pay. But potential loss of life was not something they took lightly. NASA requires that each astronaut confront the risks of his or her mission with reality thinking and ensures that they are prepared to go into outer space with the clear understanding that they may not return. The astronauts must "have their affairs in order."

Evelyn Husband, wife of the late Rick Husband, knew the risks when her husband commanded the shuttle *Columbia*. On February 1, 2003, her greatest fears came true when the shuttle exploded on reentering the earth's atmosphere. Her husband and the father of her children would never come home.

She shared with me her experience of grief:

"We were in Florida, waiting in the stands at the landing site with Rick's mom, brother, and my children. About a minute prior to landing we could tell by looking at everybody that something was horrifically wrong. I asked one of the astronauts who was with me, 'When are we supposed to hear the sonic boom?' And then I heard Rick's brother say, 'We're not going to hear a sonic boom.'

"February 1st was the worst day of my life. But I ran into God's arms and hung on tightly, and He hung on tight back to me. I knew that I could rest in His strength. I've looked all through the Bible to see if there's a loophole where you can get out of mourning, and you can't. I have to go through this whether I like it or not, but I cannot tell you what an amazing thing it is to have God's joy and peace amidst absolute sorrow."

Despite her grief, Evelyn expressed no regrets that her husband had chosen the wrong profession or dreamed the wrong dream. Instead, she explained to me that Rick's priorities were in order when he made the decision to become an astronaut, and they remained in the right order as he strived to reach that dream.

"He wanted to be an astronaut since he was four years of age. That was his life goal. I met Rick in college, and we dated all through school. I watched as every choice he made in his career was pointing toward fulfilling every box he needed to check off on that astronaut application. It was interesting that when Rick finally had all of the criteria to become an astronaut, God was really working on him, asking him, 'Rick, what are the desires of your heart?' Rick's knee-jerk answer was always, 'I want to be an astronaut.' God persevered with

Rick, and finally Rick took it to the deeper level so that his desire was to serve God, to love Him with all of his heart, to be a good husband and a good father. Once Rick came to that realization, he applied and God rewarded him with becoming an astronaut after he had his priorities set.

"He very much put God first, us second, and his job third. He had a very cool job—he loved his job—but it wasn't everything to him. Jesus was everything to him. When you make Jesus everything to you, everything else falls into place. I'm so thankful for the legacy that Rick has left us with. He set an example for our children. That's a legacy that I hope will continue throughout their lives—about putting Jesus first and relying on Him.

"Most people don't actually think about death before it occurs, even though it's going to happen to all of us. I think we're in denial over it. But at NASA they fill out a sheet with all of their financial and personal requests just in case a mission fails. On Rick's sheet, they found his personal notes for a funeral service. All Rick wrote was, 'Tell them about Jesus, because He's real to me.'"

For most of us, our jobs don't carry the dangers associated with being an astronaut, but all of us face risks, seen and unseen, in everyday situations.

Confronting life's risks with realistic possibility thinking will challenge you at many different turns. But how do you know if the risk you are engaging in is worth it?

How do you confront risks, both actual and potential? To begin with, face them honestly and positively. Don't be blinded by unreasonable illusions of risk-free rewards. Before you get in the game, find out what you will have to pay to play.

Unless and until you stand up to the dangers—real or imagined—you are not in the game of life. Seek out wise and responsible positive thinkers for counsel. Ask them the unpleasant questions. "Is there anything wrong with this that I haven't thought about?" "Is there an exit strategy you could recommend in an emergency?" "Are there midflight corrections I could make without aborting the mission?"

But know for sure that you will certainly lose if you refuse to pay the price. Practice realistic possibility thinking. Put on a parachute. Buy insurance. Get a good lawyer. Bolster your defenses. Then go for the adventure.

At the emotionally tender age of thirteen, when most teenagers are worried about acne or body shape, young Erik Weihenmayer faced a life-changing disease that left him blind. But the teenager's desire to live life fully with or without his sight enabled him to focus on a future instead of on failure.

Realistic possibility thinking is what enabled Erik to be the first blind person to climb to the top of Mount Everest. Erik's dream to reconnect with the world in a tangible way was not without dangers. Yet his goal of living life fully despite his blindness allowed him to confront the risks with a "how can I make it happen" attitude.

"We can't control all of the things that happen to us," Erik told me, "but we can make our lives whatever we want them to be. I didn't want to squander my life. Life's a gift—I wanted to live it as fully as I could."

So Erik tried to defy the odds and live a "normal" life. But it wasn't until he took up the sport of rock climbing that he found his calling. "There wasn't a baseball to hit me in the head," he explained. "I could grab these holes and scan my hands up the face of the rocks. It was so tactile; it was almost painful, like a rebirth. I felt, this is what connects me to the world.

"My friend and I were rock climbing in Arizona one day, and he said, 'Why don't we climb something a little bigger?' I said, 'Like what—you mean a 200-foot rock face?' And he said, 'How about Mount McKinley—the tallest peak in North America?'"

So Erik put his dream to the test. "I don't consider myself a crazy risk taker," he said, "but you can't avoid some of those leaps of faith. I went out and trained a lot and climbed lots of smaller mountains. The next year I became the first blind person to stand on the summit of Mount McKinley, the top of North America."

Erik explained that as he subsequently climbed all seven of the tallest peaks on each of the seven continents in the world, including Mount Everest, he did so because of the support of friends from around the world and his faith. Taking that "leap of faith" enabled him to find strength in himself that he never thought he had. "I'm not that strong," he contended.

"Twenty years ago, after I went blind, I would have been thankful to find the bathroom by myself. On the summit of

Everest, I said a prayer and thanked God for everything I have. Some people say your cup is half full or half empty—my cup is overflowing. Coming home was great because life is full of achievement, but it's also full of joy with my family. My wife and I were married on Mount Kilimanjaro in Africa. When I was thirteen, I realized that blindness isn't a death sentence. I wanted to live life fully. I wanted to have a family. I didn't want to be swept aside and forgotten. I paid the price and the reward has been fantastic!"

Not to dare to face risks may be the greatest risk of all!

I have observed in a lifetime of engaging my dream that the first question most decisionmakers are tempted to ask is: What will it cost? Asking that question at the onset, in my opinion, can be a terrible mistake. The question will be appropriate later, but as the first question it is premature. For the answer is all too often too heavy to be handled at this stage. Again and again the costs in available resources—both financial (dollars) and human (time, emotion, and talent)—may not match the mission challenge.

The first question—or questions—must qualify and quantify the passion for your project. Your dream must be strongly reaffirmed before the cost is counted and the risks must be measured against the potential rewards that are promised. A sign over the old tailor's bench reads: "Measure three times, but cut only once."

In my ministry I present new projects to my church board members by first instructing them, "Do not ask, 'What will it cost?' until you address and answer these three questions:

1. "Would it be a great thing for God? If we are not unanimous with the answer yes, then we'll spend no more time thinking about it. If the answer is yes, we will ask the second question.

2. "Would it help human beings who need help? Again, the unanimous answer must be yes or we'll forget it. If the answer is yes, we'll ask the third question.

3. "Is anybody else already doing the job? If the answer is yes, we may take another look at who and what is being done before we move with it. If the answer is no—no one is doing anything about it—then we'll consider a motion to proceed, carefully and prayerfully.

When you've done that as wisely as possible, then it's time to ask the questions: What will it cost? What are the risks and rewards of the mission?

Count the costs. Are you ready for this engagement? Before you make an irretrievable commitment, ask the wise questions: Is this a mission I should connect to? Does this mission fit in with my values and priorities? Your personal values must be clean and clear of confusion as you determine the price you can and should consider paying in pursuing your life's mission.

• • •

As you enter the stimulating arena of risk-taking, know that some risks should be labeled "nonnegotiable." Nonnegotiable risks should consider your faith, your country, your family relationships, your financial integrity, and your self-respect.

Risks that are to be counted as nonnegotiable also include your reputation. Kathy Ireland pursued her mission in modeling and reached the pinnacle of fame and fortune. I was honored to introduce her on our television program because she is a wonderful role model. Her book *Powerful Inspirations: Eight Lessons That Will Change Your Life* is a must-read for all teenage girls. This is what Kathy told our audience:

"I was modeling in Paris, and it sounds a lot more glamorous than it was. I was staying in a home where I didn't feel comfortable, so basically after work I would lock myself in my room. And it was out of boredom, loneliness, and jet lag that I picked up a Bible my mom had packed in my suitcase, and for some reason I opened it up to the Gospels and I started reading. And as I read I was just blown away. As an eighteen-year-old, I'm reading about Jesus, and He was really cool. He wasn't anything like I thought. He wasn't out there condemning. He was loving and leading.

"Here I was, a young woman for the first time on my own, but in a world that oftentimes felt dominated by men. And when I read how Jesus loves and respects every person I was so encouraged. During biblical times, in a time and a place where women were not even considered second-class citizens, Jesus gave them honor, dignity, and self-respect. Then and there I became a Christian. *He became my best Friend. That relationship helped me not to compromise.*"

That strength to hold firm served Kathy well one day when a photographer said, "Take your blouse off."

"I had had several uncomfortable situations, and this was one of them. When the photographer asked me to pose without a shirt on, I explained to him I didn't feel comfortable posing like that. He became very pushy, and he crossed that line with me. Actually he gave me a physical shove. I'm not a violent person, but I had to give him a shove back, and I walked off the job. But the courage of knowing that God was with me gave me the strength and courage to walk away from any situation. And I knew that with Him with me I could do something else for a living."

That became a defining moment in the shaping of Kathy Ireland's life's mission. Today she is the dynamic CEO of a billion-dollar business. And Kathy has been happily married for over sixteen years and is the mother of three children.

Kathy describes her wish for her children this way:

"They grow and get to an age where they start to question authority, and they realize that maybe Mom and Dad don't really know everything. I want them to have their own relationship with Jesus. I want them, as they're questioning authority, to turn to God, because He is the Ultimate Authority. And it is my prayer for them that they would stay on His path."

• • •

Fame and fortune can be very alluring, but they demand a price. Too many people who attain great wealth become intoxicated by it, and in time they are "ripped off" by exploiters, their fortune wasted, stolen, or simply mismanaged into oblivion. Five men I know personally have lost over $1 billion *each* in *one year's* time.

Fame and fortune also carry unpredictable risks for relationships. Are your friends really friends, or are they after your money? "Celebritism" is big in America. But the face or name that has become celebrated is going to be solicited for good or ill.

If you serve in a public position—for example, as a TV anchor, a politician, an entertainer, an athlete, or, yes, even a preacher—you lose your privacy, and with it the freedom to go anywhere, anytime, to just enjoy yourself with your spouse or a close family member or friend. As many celebrities have said to me, "Fame can make you feel more like a product than a person."

But every mission demands that a price be paid. "No man will ever build a tower without counting the cost," Jesus said (Luke 14:28). There are the upfront costs that are relatively easy to estimate—the price of tools, instruments, education, degrees, permits, or plans. In the early stage of engagement this is called "front money."

The late Dave Thomas, founder of the Wendy's restaurant chain, was a friend and fellow member of the Horatio Alger Society Association. He knew that both the financial and emotional risks would be great when he sought to realize his lifelong dream of starting his own company. He had learned early on that it takes hard work to succeed in any competitive field.

At the age of fifteen, Dave was already tired of moving from state to state with his adoptive stepfamily, so he stayed behind in Knoxville, Tennessee, living at the local YMCA and supporting himself with a job at the local Hobby House restaurant. "I learned quickly that if I didn't work, I wouldn't be able to eat," he said. That hard work was a foretaste of the future.

After a stint in the Army, Dave continued in the restaurant business, working his way up from short-order cook to vice president of the Hobby House chain in Fort Wayne. It was then that he had the opportunity to take over a failing Kentucky Fried Chicken franchise in Columbus, Ohio, for a payout of an ownership percentage. The financial picture was bleak, but the risk was primarily his time and energy. Accepting the risk and pursuing his dream, Dave met the challenge head-on. Not only did he turn the franchise around, but he went on to add more franchises, eventually selling them for $1.5 million.

Still dreaming of having his own company, Dave opened the first Wendy's Old Fashioned Hamburgers in Columbus in 1969. His popular restaurant expanded quickly. In 1973 Dave took on the financial risk of borrowing $1 million in order to sell franchises. The risk was well managed, however: Dave carefully selected his franchisees from people who were very experienced in restaurant operations. In the first one hundred months, more than one thousand units opened. By 1979 annual sales had reached $1 billion.

Dave Thomas's success enabled him to fulfill his even greater passion—to actively support various charitable and educational organizations. With his wife, Lorraine, whom he met at the Hobby House in Fort Wayne, Dave had a large family of his own, including five children and six grandchildren. He never forgot his orphaned roots and worked hard until his death to help disadvantaged children.

It all was possible because he was able to face his risks with realistic positive thinking.

The cost of every mission should be calculated in terms of not only money but also the personal investment of time and emotional energy. What price are you willing to pay? What sacrifices are you willing to make? It is imperative that you estimate the stress and strain on your valued relationships. Your passion to pursue your calling will have a bearing on your marriage, family, and friends.

Will the hoped-for rewards be worth those risks? Here are some wise questions that should be answered before you put yourself, your family, or your position at risk of failure.

1. Is the timing right? Will it be to your advantage to wait? Will the opportunity still be there in a year? Or years from now? Will the price go down if you delay the commitment, or will the costs rise?

2. Do you need to reprioritize your priorities? Should you put this new engagement at the top of your priorities and lower other priorities to which you are committed?

3. Can you live with failure in this cause? What if you pay the price only to reap rewards that are less than expected and not worth the price you paid?

4. Would you feel pride in honorable failure? Will people say, "He had the courage to try"? "He was ahead of his time, but he broke new ground"? "He was faithful to his mission"?

5. Before you assume responsibility for the price that must be paid or the risks you must assume, ask yourself, "What's the worst that can happen? Can I handle that eventuality?"

6. Are you wisely managing your ego? That question helps you keep a tiger-eye on your God-given goal. You want to be able to sincerely say, "I'm not ego-driven—I'm success-focused," and, "I don't want my own way; I just don't want to make mistakes of omission or commission." But be wise here: the fear of an ego-shattering failure can keep you from facing potentially rewarding risks. By contrast, an inflated ego that ignores the possibility of failure can lead to disaster.

7. Can you pass on some of the risks to someone else?
   Can you connect with someone who is more
   sophisticated, more experienced, or more creatively
   empowered to take or share specific risks?

As I faced my life's mission, I focused on the enormous possible risks I would have to manage creatively or run the risk of aborting my mission. What would that failure cost me? One idea gave me the courage to face my risk of failure: *I'd rather attempt to do something great and fail than attempt to do nothing and succeed.*

When I arrived in California at the age of twenty-eight, I had accepted the call to begin a new church. With only two members—Mrs. Schuller and myself—and only $500 in cash in the mission's bank account, I faced the fact that there were no empty halls on Sunday mornings where I could hold services. But rising to the challenge, I hit upon the only place where we could meet—a drive-in theater. "Yes," the owner said, smiling with that "now I've heard everything" look in his eye. "But I'll have to charge you $10 to pay the sound man."

I was enthused. I could cover this cost out of the morning's free-will offering. No risk here! I would simply stand on the roof of the one-story snack bar and projection booth and preach, my voice transmitted through the car speakers that visitors would place inside their windows.

On the Saturday night before the first service, I was awakened from a deep sleep. "What if it rains tomorrow morning?" I found myself asking for the first time. I hadn't thought of that! I didn't even own an umbrella. What if I were left standing there, being drenched by rain, stared at by people sitting dry in their cars, until they were forced to drive away in embarrassment for me? I prayed, "God, what will I do if it rains tomorrow? How can I be sure I won't look like a fool? How do I prepare for this risk?"

God answered my prayer with a powerful positive idea. "Schuller, don't worry about the weather. That's my responsibility, not yours. You deliver the message. Make it great! That's your responsibility!"

I relaxed completely. That first Sunday, and every Sunday for the next five years, I preached under the open sky and *never once* worried about the weather! The only risk was that I might deliver a message that would bomb out, but that was a risk I could manage.

As a young minister, I learned one of the most important lessons for anyone facing risks in their desire to succeed: *focus on the risks that are your sole responsibility.*

But also be ready to ask for help. Be prepared to share the risk and the glory with others. Let me revise an earlier statement: *God can do terrific things through the person who will generously share the credit.*

My life has been completely consumed by the faith that there is a God who gave me my mission. I trust that He will guide me, giving me the wisdom to make the right decisions at the right time. Here is the truth behind the fifty-year story of my life's mission: the right people came into my life at the right time, and with the right resources. Again and again, people came to my attention from "out of the blue," bringing skills, talents, knowledge, connections, money, and management experience. I neither knew them nor selected them. How did I find them? Divine Providence is the only answer!

There is one last thing to keep in mind when counting up the cost of your mission: you must embrace your mission with courage in your heart.

Dare to try. Dare to love. Dare to make a commitment. Dare to take a risk.

If you don't dare to take a risk, you'll never really *live*. You'll throw away all of your tomorrows.

To laugh is to risk appearing the fool.

To weep is to risk appearing sentimental.

To reach for another is to risk involvement.

To expose your feelings is to risk exposing your true self.

To place your ideas, your dreams, before a crowd is to risk their loss.

To love is to risk not being loved in return.

To live is to risk dying.

To believe is to risk despair.

To try is to risk failure.

But risks must be taken, because the greatest hazard in life is to risk nothing.

The people who risk nothing do nothing, have nothing, and are nothing.

They may avoid suffering and sorrow, but they cannot learn, feel, change, grow, love, live.

Chained by their attitudes, they are slaves; they have forfeited their freedom.

Only a person who risks is free.

SEVEN

Stay Focused on
Your Dreams

Faith plus *focus* plus *follow-through*
equals *mission accomplished!*

In earlier writings I shared an idea with you: *faith* plus *focus* plus *follow-through* equals *success.* Now I would like to revise the final word of that line so that it reads: *faith* plus *focus* plus *follow-through* equals . . . *mission accomplished.*

Goals reached; desires fulfilled; success achieved; purpose realized; vision experienced; mission accomplished; dreams coming true: however you put it, the secret in making success happen is often found in this one discipline "focus."

In this chapter, let's *focus* on "focus." To focus is to turn your well-defined mission into a determined, destiny-directing goal. It means to passionately concentrate your creative energy on the bull's-eye of your target.

As a child growing up on an Iowa farm, I remember the special times in the fall, when there were the bonfires and marshmallow roasts. All the leaves were raked and piled together with the dead sticks. Then Dad would say, "Who is going to light the bonfire?" "I will! I will!" was my eager response and I would get my small magnifying glass to focus the sun's rays onto a dried leaf. We would all watch as a small spiral of smoke would soon drift upward and then a bright yellow flame.

Something like that happens when the variety of talents, passions, and values that swirl within a single human mind come together. When these forces become a creative coalition, focused and magnified on an inspiring dream, they release tremendous energy. When you bring together positive emotions and passionately focus them on your goal, you create consuming, burning drive.

Then the vision becomes a venture!

But staying focused is a continuing challenge. The serious athlete wrestles with staying focused when his friends invite him to join them at the beach for a weekend of fun. The aspiring pianist focuses on long hours at the piano instead of watching entertaining television programs. Early morning practices conflict with sleeping an extra hour. Hours of concentrated study and work can quickly squelch enthusiasm, unless the focus from start to finish is on the goal and the mission is accomplished. Otherwise, a multitude of distractions will siphon off your energy and drive.

When you announce your new and exciting dream with

friends and family, do not be surprised if they do not immediately share your enthusiasm. Your new goals may compete with their spoken or unspoken plans. They may have their own agenda that they hope will gain your support.

So be on guard—listen and learn from them—but keep your eye focused on your goal. Be prepared too for possible opposition. Some people will bring to your idea values that collide or conflict with yours. Your good idea may encounter obstacles thrown up by people for different reasons. Some may intend to obstruct you, while others—your friends—really care about you and are trying to keep you from making mistakes. A strong ego can become a dangerous ego. But stay focused on your mission by telling yourself this truth: every good idea has problems and needs improvement. Listen. Learn. Adjust. Adapt. Improve. Make corrections. Remember the line I gave you earlier, "Measure three times, but cut only once."

Stay focused! You alone have the power to defeat your dream. Rejection is never a fatal or final problem unless and until you yourself reject your mission.

Detractors—they will be there. But detractors must not become distracters. Simply *stay* focused and sell your ideas positively. Your positive passion can be infectious! Enthusiasm has fabulous power to attract support from hesitant listeners. New encouragers will emerge from the shadows to sustain and support you!

• • •

Polio was a horrendous, debilitating, and often-fatal disease that became an epidemic in the early twentieth century. The best and brightest medical researchers universally failed in their effort to make breakthroughs—until Dr. Jonas Salk found the cure for this global plague.

I was seated near this great scientist at a luncheon one day when he shared with those of us at his table about his detractors: "When I first shared my ideas, my scientific associates rejected them outright with one unanimous word: 'impossible.' As I reported new evidence that I uncovered in my ongoing research and my theories were strengthened, some of them were asked what they thought of my work, and they answered, 'We do not support him—but his ideas are interesting.' Others simply slipped into the shadows and argued with their friends against my work behind my back. But no one asked one sincere question or offered support or encouragement. I was left alone. I stayed focused. When the vaccination became an uncontroversial success, I read their quotes in papers, 'I believed long ago that he was on to something!' But not one of my earlier detractors ever said, 'He was right, I was wrong!'"

A creative mind does not stop conceiving new creative concepts just because it is committed to a single mission. Delicious distractions can dangerously divert even the boldest dreamer. These positive distractions come in the form of good ideas, either your own or those brought to you by others. But these ideas, however good they are, become deceptively dangerous if they compete for the time, energy, and resources available for your central mission. Stay focused.

One of the most inspiring achievers I know is LuAnn Mitchell. A farmer's daughter, she was confronted at the age of sixteen with an unwanted pregnancy for which she was not responsible. But she didn't let that stop her. Later she was blessed when she fell in love and married Fred Mitchell. His goal was to build a great meat business, marketing to Canadian retailers. Almost immediately he faced opposition from all areas, even his mother and sister, who sued him to try to take over his business. But LuAnn and her husband were a strong team and won in court. The business began to flourish. Then, with hundreds of employees, they developed an aggressive expansion plan for their business. They needed $30 million in new capital. That was more than their bank could offer. A dead end? No—they decided to go public and sell stock in a bold new IPO. They stayed on target as they worked through all the impossibilities to get the necessary permits for their fast-growing company.

Before the IPOs could be signed, a potentially fatal illness befell LuAnn's husband. The prognosis was grim. Only a heart and lung transplant could save Fred's life. In 1990 doctors in Stanford, California, performed the then-rare heart and lung transplant surgery. The procedure was a success, and Fred Mitchell's recovery was exceptional.

Through all these difficult times, Fred and LuAnn stayed focused by watching my television program, *The Hour of Power*, every Sunday in their Canadian home. They wrote me and offered to share how their faith had pulled them through. Fred Mitchell was the first heart-transplant recipient to be my guest in the Crystal Cathedral. What an inspiration!

Now that he was healthy again, Fred felt confident that he could sign the IPO documents and that the business they had started from scratch could boom. But just before the company was to be listed on the stock exchange, Fred went in for a routine medical checkup at Stanford.

At the Stanford clinic he was led into the examination room. "You can wait here, Mrs. Mitchell," the doctors instructed her. "It won't be long. He's in great shape." LuAnn waited . . . and waited. When it seemed to her that the exam was taking too long, without invitation or approval she bounded through the unlocked door of the surgical ward. Inside the room was chaos. The doctors were frantically trying to revive her husband. He had collapsed without warning or reason. Fred Mitchell was dead.

LuAnn returned home to Canada and on her way to the funeral of her husband, she was asked to attend an emergency meeting. There, dressed in her mourning clothes with her children accompanying her, she was confronted by a corporate board that had privately agreed that she would be replaced. "LuAnn," they announced, "we have good news for you at this tragic time. We have agreed to buy your stock, relieve you of the burden of becoming the CEO, and replace you. You'll be safe and secure. We promise." She was stunned. She was angry. She and her husband together had built the company. It was their life. She couldn't just walk away. "I am not selling out to you guys," she screamed. Her clenched fist pounded the table before their unbelieving eyes. "Mr. Mitchell and I built this. I lost my husband, but

I will not allow what we built to die with him. I owe that to him."

LuAnn remained focused in spite of the horrendous obstacles before her. In two days the IPO permit would expire unless she signed the documents. "I can do it," she said. Suddenly she was seized by a powerful intuition. "Don't sign it" was the message she heard. But then what? She prayed and got guidance. LuAnn conceived a daring idea: orchestrate a strategic merger with a competing firm! That would make the business a national marketing force to create hundreds of new jobs. She met with the CEO of the competition and they decided that it could be win-win for everyone. That's focus! Three months later they signed the deal. The merger was a fantastic success.

After four more successful years, and with the blessing of her employees, LuAnn Mitchell sold her interest in the company to her partner. "Now I can walk away. My husband and I pulled it off." The sale of her stock left her very wealthy and free to move on to another mission—philanthropy.

What happens when "interruptions" come to take your focus off your mission and your tomorrows? I was in Amsterdam at our ministry's office, planning to leave the next day for an appointment with Pope John Paul II at the Vatican. From there I would leave for Russia and our ministry's office in Moscow. I was picked up at the Amsterdam airport by the head of my Dutch office. As I climbed into the front seat of his car, I bumped my head on the door frame. I said, "Ouch," and thought that was that.

By the time my dinner meeting was through, my headache was so severe that I excused myself to "sleep it off." I stopped at the concierge for aspirin. He gave me a plastic box containing four. I took all four pills, not knowing that I had broken a blood vessel in my brain and the aspirin would thin my blood and cause dangerously severe bleeding. I took a hot bath. Then I slipped into bed, not knowing that I was already on the edge of a coma.

The next morning, when I didn't show up or answer the telephone, my traveling companions came to look for me. They found me near death on the balcony of my room overhanging the canal. Fortunately, I had collapsed backward against the door. Had I fallen forward, the low ornamental railing would not have prevented me from falling into the water below. But my body had wedged against the door, preventing my searching staff from being able to open it and rescue me. They used a ladder to create a bridge from the balcony of the next room.

I was taken to a hospital, where a neurosurgeon shaved my hair, lifted my scalp, and proceeded to saw through the skull bone in an attempt to stop the bleeding. The operation was only partly successful. But after a second surgery I was on my way to recovery. The neurosurgeon told us that had the bleeding gone unchecked for another twenty minutes, I would have died.

It was several days before I could focus my injured brain to think clearly. But the very first thought that came was a God-thought: "How sweet it is to stand on the edge of tomorrow!" While I was in surgery, my associates called Rome and Russia to cancel my appointments. Now that's what I call an interruption!

There are times when God requires you to make a midflight correction. It can seem devastating at the time, but it allows God to redirect or reaffirm you to empower you to focus on your tomorrows.

Gracia and Martin Burham were Christian missionaries, sharing their love for God with people in the outermost parts of the world. Their dedication to their mission was clear and steadfast. They were focused on spreading the Gospel. No one foresaw the tragedy that was about to befall them.

As missionary pilots in the Philippines, they chose to celebrate their wedding anniversary on one of the beautiful outer islands.

Much later, at the Crystal Cathedral, Gracia Burham described their celebration. "We went to an island resort called Dos Palmas. Everyone had told us how great this resort was. One night, a little before dawn, there was a *bang-bang-bang* on the door. I thought maybe a guard was drunk. Martin headed for the door, but before he could get there, three men with M-16s broke the door down and came into the room.

"They pointed their guns at me and said, 'Go, go, go!' I said, 'No, I'm not dressed.' I was grabbing my things, and when I finally got something on, they took us out to a speed-boat. As we were taken away, along with eighteen other hostages, the men raised their weapons in the air and yelled, 'Allah Akbar!' We knew then it was the Abu Sayyaf—a familiar name in the Philippines, known as a radical Muslim terrorist, extremist group believed to have ties to Al-Quaeda."

For the next twelve months the terrorists forced the Burhams to run for their lives as the Philippine military pursued them. Gun battle after gun battle ensued. They were either running or where the terrorists thought they were in a safe place, away from the military, where there was nothing to do. Gracia said, "We lived in either extreme terror or extreme boredom. There was no in-between at all. We were often sick, suffering from diarrhea, and at the same time there was never enough food."

Gracia went on to describe her captors' motives. "They had resorted to kidnapping for ransom to finance their jihad, their holy war. But they said, 'You're Americans. We'll make political demands and get concessions for you. We'll take care of you.'"

It became clear to the Burhams that the terrorists wanted ransom or they would not be released. The terrorists traveled from village to village, but there was no money waiting so there was no release.

"Finally, after about one year, a ransom was paid for us," Gracia said, "and even though we started to be fed better, the terrorists told us, 'A ransom has been paid, but we're going to ask for more.' I begged them not to do that. I said, 'This will not turn out well.' But they asked for more, and more ransom money never came."

Finally, the missionaries' worst fear came true. There was another gun battle, which proved to be the final one between the military and the terrorists: "One afternoon it was starting to rain, so we set up our hammocks and shelters to keep us dry. We didn't know the military had been following our footprints all day. They came over the hill, saw our camp, and opened fire. Martin was shot immediately. I was in the hammock beside him, and I was hit too. I looked at Martin, and he was bleeding from the chest. Then I heard him breathe very deeply, like in a deep sleep, and soon his body sagged against mine. I knew he was dead. The Lord gave me such grace right there in that moment. I felt God's peace and I've felt it ever since. Then I heard the sound of an approaching helicopter, and I was rescued. Today my wounds are healed and I have a faith like I never had before this jungle experience. I would never wish that on anyone, but you know, the Lord brings good things out of everything."

While Martin and Gracia were held captive, their thoughts turned to planning for the worst. "We talked about every scenario when we were in the jungle . . . what I was supposed to do if Martin didn't come home and I did. He even told me who he wanted to preach at his funeral, and we had the neatest God-honoring funeral for him. He told me what kind of car to buy, how much to put down, and how much to borrow. I knew what Martin wanted because we had talked about it so many times."

Today Gracia is refocusing her mission without her husband, still focused on the goals of the mission they shared when they were together—sharing the love of God with others. Some might say that the tragedy has enabled both of the Burhams to have a more far-reaching impact: Martin through death, and Gracia through surviving. Yet they are unquestionably still together spiritually.

Few of us will suffer the way the Burhams did during their terrifying ordeal. Their supernatural ability to survive the most horrific conditions is a testimony to the power and peace of prayer. But while we may not be captured by terrorists in our lives, we do need to resist the captivity of naysayers, pessimists, detractors, and disappointers.

Distractions, disappointments, and interruptions can be expected during the long process of living out your life's dream. When downtimes come, when your early enthusiasm diminishes and sometimes disappears through the energy-draining frustrations in the process, then you need to stay focused. Dig in. Never quit. Hold on. Never give up.

Time and again you may suffer from the loss of a relationship that is vital to your career. Not all of your trusted and helpful colleagues will remain at your side. Some may die, others will not be on the same page with you. They will slip away. Then unexpected problems arise, arguments and disagreements happen. Obstacles and obstructions emerge, sometimes from nowhere. Expect the early excitement of your purposeful mission to diminish with time, but you must stay focused!

How do you handle the downtimes when your enthusiasm begins to lose momentum? Pick up the theme of the possibility thinkers' creed: "I will not quit!" Pump up the positive spirit by going to the window at the beginning of the day, looking at the new sunrise, and affirming out loud, "I believe! I believe! I believe!" Do it faithfully, daily, and regularly. Affirm it as you put your head on the pillow at the end of the day. "I believe, I believe, I believe!" *Stay focused* on the dream!

This book is my testimony. I've been there in the past half century. This is not a report on my research— this is a true story of how I made my dreams come true.

There are four essential ingredients that worked for me and helped me to stay focused on my life's dream through difficult and sometimes dangerous detours.

1. *Passion:* Any dream, mission, or, yes, even marriage can lose the passion you felt when you first said yes to it. Keep the passion alive with emotionally fulfilling moments that rekindle the positive feelings that led you down this path initially. Initiate romance even when you don't feel it. In your mission, keep inspiring mementos around you, like a copy of your first paycheck or photos of significant milestones. Celebrate each anniversary of your commitment, your marriage, or your business. Emotionalize the journey.

2. *Patience:* Our culture of instant gratification fuels impatience. It used to take days to have film developed. Then

we had one-day service, followed by one-hour service. Now we have instant development with digital cameras. Have we forgotten how to wait? This one word is used throughout the Bible. "Wait on the Lord." "Trust and wait on God." We need faith to keep focused.

3. *Persistence and perseverance:* These are the powerful keys to success in all of living. Jim Nicholson was a farm boy who lived in abject poverty just a few miles from where I grew up. He lived in an abandoned farmhouse because his mother could not afford to pay rent. He was teased because he never had a matching pair of shoes. His father, an alcoholic, was nowhere to be found, but Jim's mother kept her two young sons focused on positive goals. She would tell them, "You can do and be anything you want to be. Forget the teasing. Don't let anyone stop you from achieving your goals." Through hard work and focus, this mother's dreams for her sons came true when Jim's older brother was accepted at the U.S. Military Academy. Meanwhile, Jim, at the age of fifteen, worked odd jobs to help earn enough money to buy his brother's train ticket to West Point. He continued to work hard and study as he stayed focused for West Point also. He succeeded, then went on to law school and a fabulous career as a land developer. Today, Jim Nicholson is financially independent and serves in the honored position of U.S. ambassador to the Vatican!

4. *Providence:* Expect God's divine intervention. Look for

it and recognize it when it happens. In times of deep frustration, when you cannot handle the pain or persecution or apparent failure, give God a chance to turn the obstacle into a new opportunity.

On September 24, 2000, Laura Wilkinson achieved what had looked to be impossible: she won the coveted gold medal on her high dive in the Olympics in Sydney, Australia. And she did it with a broken foot.

Laura broke three bones in her foot during a routine dry-land training session only twelve weeks before the team trials. She thought her Olympic goals were crushed as well, but before she knew it she was in Sydney as a member of the U.S. Olympic diving team. With her foot in a cast, Laura couldn't train in the pool. Instead, her coach critiqued her as she stood on the diving board, made arm motions, and went through the dives in her head. She now sees that as a blessing in disguise.

"When I broke my foot, *I lost my focus*, I wanted to be back in the water. But 'pretend diving' helped me remember how much I loved what I did." Laura, her doctor, and her coach together designed a special shoe for her to wear when climbing the high-dive ladder. Before every dive and practice, Laura recited her favorite Bible verse, "I can do all things with Christ who strengthens me" (Philippians 4:13). This verse had been her theme through her growing-up years. In eighth grade she had even "lived" in a shirt with that verse printed on it.

In the final rounds of her Olympic competition Laura rose from eighth place. In the fourth round, she suddenly faced overwhelming fear! Her coach said to her, "Laura, do this dive for Hillary," a close friend who had been killed in a car accident. Laura took the focus off herself and decided, "This is for God. This is for all my friends." Suddenly it wasn't so scary anymore. She limped in pain to the top of the ladder, where she took off her "handicapped" shoe and threw it down to her coach. She balanced on the ball of her broken foot, prayed her silent prayer, then jumped and completed the dive that won the first U.S. gold medal in over thirty years in the ten-meter platform dive in Women's Olympic competitions. Her first words to a reporter after she won were the words from Philippians that had kept her so focused: "I can do all things with Christ who strengthens me."

Laura experienced *faith* plus *focus* plus *follow-through* equals *a dream realized.*

Years ago I penned what I call the Possibility Thinker's Creed. It sums up how I interpret the word *focus.*

When faced with a mountain,
I will not quit!
I will keep on striving
until I climb over,
find a pass through,
tunnel underneath,
or simply stay and
turn the mountain into a gold mine,
with God's help!

EIGHT

Choose and Clear the Channels of Communication

Your network will make success work.

"Do you think, Dr. Schuller, that I might be in the early stages of Alzheimer's disease?" The young man before me was very stressed. His eyes were wide with worry.

"How old are you, Mark?" I asked, guessing he was less than thirty.

"I'm going to be thirty in three weeks," he answered. His voice showed a twinge of anxiety, as if that ominous number marked him as leaving youth forever behind, with old age waiting quietly and impolitely around the bend.

"Well, I think you're too young to be worried about Alzheimer's. What makes you so concerned?" I asked.

"I feel I'm losing my memory. I can't remember names and dates like I used to." He rattled off illustrations. It was what I had been hearing from my own five children—all past thirty. Instinctively I answered him.

"Mark, you're not losing normal memory capability—you're suffering from overload." I explained further. "The memory system on your mental computer has a load limit. Pointing to my tape recorder, I said, "Just like that tape in my machine. It records only two hours. Your mind has a load limit too. When God created human beings in the Garden of Eden, voice to ear was the only channel for communication. Now fast-forward to today. Technology, which has no manners, abruptly interrupts spoken conversations.

"I deal with this every day, Mark. I will be in the middle of a face-to-face conversation with my wife and suddenly the phone will ring and break into my train of thought. I hang up and ask, 'Where were we?' Add to the uninvited telephone interruption the intrusions of radio and television. We also now have a fax machine. And here comes the Internet and e-mail. The doorbell rings, and it's Federal Express with something that just can't wait. And every day I have to double-check: 'Oh, the mailbox hasn't been emptied yet. It's full of—' what do we call all that 'stuff'? Junk mail? Plus bills, first-class letters, invitations to a variety of events. Oh, yes, by letter and brochure we get messages to remind us to answer that letter we were sent earlier.

"There goes the *ding-a-ling*. It sounds pleasant enough. It's my cell phone. As I answer, I see a fax coming through. I search for the fresh paper message and place it on the other papers that came in just over the last twenty-four hours. A strange feeling comes over me, and I feel trapped by all these 'messages.' I'm feeling—overwhelmed! And this is all one day's collection. There was yesterday, and the day before, and tomorrow is only hours away, with wave after wave already on the way. *Overload!*

"On top of all that, Mark," I continued, "you're not a teenager anymore. Each day and every year, your mind will be loaded down with more names, more places, and more numbers you'll have to remember . . . new birthdays . . . anniversaries . . . more invitations to special events. The load will get larger and heavier each year you add to your life. Warning! You'll be tempted to lock the door to tomorrow.

"And you're living in America in the twenty-first century," I added. "Shopping malls and stores are open seven days a week. Sundays are busier than ever. When I was a child, Sundays were quiet days for church and family. Today it's for not only baseball but the NFL, NBA, NHL, plus soccer moms and NASCAR dads. In many a garage there is more than one car. We are living on a fast track in America. The auto used to be a quiet place, a retreat and respite from communication. But today, not only the radio but the telephone is with us in our car, and when we get home there is the TV programmed to all the new channels so we won't miss the latest headlines. All this adds to the sensory overload."

The result? Many, like Mark, are infected with the epidemic fear of early Alzheimer's.

Mental overload can lead quickly to memory problems. When we are overloaded, we don't listen. We really don't want any more information to assimilate and we settle for sound bites. Our limited brains want to shout out, "I don't want to add to the overload, I just want to unload what I feel. Now you have to listen to me!"

My advice to Mark was to try to control the overload. How? Turn off the machines periodically. Go away by yourself to a quiet place. Regroup and give your mind a rest. When I think of someone who must have been extremely overloaded, I am reminded of how sensitive and calm Jesus was when He was bombarded by people who all needed and wanted something from Him. And what would He do? He regularly went away by Himself to recharge and regroup.

Assume leadership in your life. Turn off the cell phone, let the voice mail record messages, and turn the radio down. Don't let uninvited distractions interrupt you from the more important tasks that keep you focused on your dream.

Not only are we in a battle against communication overload, but our culture has also lost its manners in conversation. People talk over each other. In groups of two, both parties are often talking at the same time. How then can we really listen and hear? Our society is suffering from communication breakdown. It's a cultural meltdown in what used to be common dignity in dialogue.

Dialogue itself is dead and dying. Dialogue used to mean an exchange of ideas, with one person speaking while others listened, and back and forth. Talk shows that started as dialogue have turned into free-for-alls. A host argues or talks over the guest who has come to be interviewed. This rudeness is a mark of cultural decline that threatens courteous communication between us as we lose the art of polite listening.

Effective communication is all important in the business of living. We need to learn sensible ways to control the channels of communications and use them not to overstress us, but to strengthen our relationship experiences. Communication is a God-given tool to establish and enjoy relationships. God designed us for relationships. "It is not good for man to live alone," He said, looking down on Adam. And God gave him Eve. Communication leads to connection, an essential need for humans.

Elie Wiesel, a survivor of the German death camps, once said something in my company that I will never forget. "I knew the worst of torture in the Holocaust," he recalled, "but the most pain and suffering I experienced there was the bleak moment when I realized no one knew where I was—dead or alive. I felt totally abandoned by all human beings. Abandonment is hell."

Relationships depend on open communication.

The basic need to communicate is so strong that it will be met even in the most desperate of circumstances. Even in the worst of times, you will, as William Faulkner said, "not only endure, but prevail." This was affirmed recently in an interview I had with an amazing man who survived six and a half years as a POW in Vietnam.

Norman McDaniel was an electronics warfare officer in the U.S. Air Force during the Vietnam War. His plane was on its fifty-first reconnaissance mission when it was shot down by enemy fire. He parachuted to the ground safely but was soon taken prisoner. He shared how the imprisonment was both brutal and torturous.

"My cell was six-by-nine and very dingy," Norman explained. "I was harassed and tortured constantly, especial during the first several months of incarceration. I was not allowed to move around in my cell much during the first few years. In fact, if the enemy caught me moving around, they would torture me and deny food and water. Time and time again I didn't know if I would live to see the next moment."

Despite being separated from all the other POWs, Norman learned that they had developed an elaborate communication network that not only allowed them to talk to each other but also provided needed support and encouragement.

"It took me about two weeks after I was captured to learn to tap code," he said. "I heard some knocking and bumping on the wall next to me when the guard was not around, but I couldn't tell what it was. Over time I figured it out, and lo and behold, the first message that came from the cell next to me was from a guy from my home state of North Carolina. That was really strengthening, really encouraging. And so we used the tap code to communicate. It was covert. If the enemy found us communicating, they would torture us severely because they knew the power and the strength of us staying in touch with each other.

"We did it anyway, at the risk and pain of torture. Each Sunday, when the Vietnamese were not around, we would covertly pass something called the church call. We had a tap signal for that. At the same time everybody would recite the Lord's Prayer, the Pledge of Allegiance, and pray for whatever they felt personally they should pray for. One of the most strengthening, most uplifting feelings was when you knew that your fellow prisoners in the next cell and in the other cell blocks were all praying at the same time."

Norman went on to describe his emotional condition, adding that to withstand the worst of the torture and separation he relied on his faith and was sustained through a higher level of communication.

"When things got really tough, I was tortured to the extent that I didn't think I could take another moment of it. The strongest source of strength came from my communication with God. I prayed from the time I was captured all the way through. I reached a closer relationship with the Lord, and a feeling of peace came that I had never experienced before and that I've never lost since. But God revealed to me that I must trust in Him in all circumstances and He will take care of the rest of it."

The six years of imprisonment left wounds that took years to heal. The toll seemed to be toughest on Norman's strength to face the emotions he had to learn to bury and control.

"The Vietnamese gave us propaganda that always made it sound bad for the United States," Norman explained. "So we would get bits and pieces of information. But when the bombings began to pick up, we began to realize that the war would probably come to an end very soon. One of the provisions of the Paris Peace Accords was that the prisoners would be notified of their release. And so we were notified. You would think that everybody would just jump up and shout, 'Hallelujah! Great! I'm going home!' Nope. We had had so many ups and downs that when they finally opened the doors to our prison cells, even though we knew it was happening, we didn't feel it. We had to control ourselves so much in that environment. If you showed any hostility toward the enemy, they would torture you and break you and make life miserable for you. We had to control our emotions to the extent that we couldn't talk about it or express it. So I had lost touch with my feelings. It wasn't until later that I began to feel that euphoria.

"When I was released, I learned that my father and my youngest sister had died while I was in captivity. I heard it, but I didn't feel it. It was two or three months later, when those feelings began to return, that I broke down and cried over the loss of my father and my sister.

"It was like coming back to life from the dead," he concluded. "It took almost two years to readjust to normal life."

Normal living for Norman McDaniel was being a part of a caring community. And a caring community is one where persons communicate kindly with one another and bridges are built. These persons are drawn closer to each other. Where there was an initial distance, now there is an emerging closeness. Eyes twinkle, faces smile, words are warm and gentle. Now creative communication happens.

The greatest challenge facing our family of humans working and living in diverse communities is the failure to communicate respectfully with each other. How do we communicate to other humans who do not agree with our views and values?

My dear friend the late Dr. Henry Poppen was a missionary in China for nearly twenty years until Mao Tse Tung's communist force came to the thriving village of Amoy and took over. For only a short time Dr. Poppen was allowed to continue his work, then suddenly he was put on public trial and imprisoned—not knowing if and when he would be executed. One night he miraculously escaped. He returned home to America and after his recovery from his imprisonment he became a copastor in our rapidly growing church. He was my mentor for the last years of his life. He was a master communicator or he would not have survived his imprisonment. He gave me these four rules of respectful communication.

1. Be friendly.

2. Be fair.

3. Be frank and then . . .

4. Be firm.

Where and how do you begin to communicate with suspicious strangers? I learned the single most successful secret from Mother Teresa. It was a sentence on a huge billboard by the airport in Calcutta, India, that all the people arriving for her funeral could not avoid seeing. Years before she had given this sentence to me personally: "Smile, it is the beginning of Peace."

In a world of conflict, new relationships with those who disagree with us certainly should not start with criticism, admonishment, scolding, rebuke, or argument. Such negative communication threatens authentic communication, for it causes emotions to be defensive, embarrassed, or angered.

I have learned a fundamental principle that I have used in my communication: always begin conversation with someone who seems to be an adversary by trying first to focus on what you can agree on—such as a common danger and your need for each other and ways of helping each other. Perhaps both of you share a positive value, like classical music or sports, or it may be moral values that you have in common. After discovering what you agree on, you are on the path to building a respectful relationship. Communication at its best always artfully and carefully seeks to seize upon areas where agreement is possible and where hopes and hurts can be shared, as well as dreams and discouragements, faith and fears. This is the emotional soil where powerful communication can happen.

I was not taught this "art" of communication when I studied to be a preacher. I was trained to preach sermons. My first year in practice I failed to win an audience. "Stop preaching and start witnessing" was a lesson I had to learn for myself. I discovered purely by accident that people don't want to be preached to; they want to be helped, honestly and sincerely.

That is the secret of effective communication. Start by being sensitive to the hurting and troubled hearts. Share how positive faith inspires, encourages, and lifts the spirit. I challenge and motivate my listeners to discover and embrace positive thinking. Every person needs that. That's the classic path to success: *Find a need and fill it. Find a hurt and heal it. Find a problem and solve it.*

When you find a disagreement, bridge it. "You shall be called a repairer of the breach and restorer of paths to dwell in" (Isaiah 58:12). This has been my lifelong guideline in communication.

Yes, my goal is not to make people feel guilty and fearful of punishment. Instead, I now target the hurts in their hearts by instilling hope, faith, and love. Believers and unbelievers alike need that. So I share true stories of inspiring faith. These true stories give courage to the fearful and hope to guilty and depressed souls. I want to share the Good News that puts happy tears in the eye and fresh dreams in the spirit.

This fundamental redefinition of my mission changed when I saw my role not as a preacher, teacher, lecturer, and evangelist, but as a communicator reporting Good News, and as a therapist using channels of communication to bring emotional healing into hurting hearts.

Are you a doctor dispensing medical aid to patients, or are you a caring physician wanting to heal? Are you a teacher standing behind a desk reciting facts to your pupils, or are you an educator understanding where the gap in each student's knowledge is? Are you a parent commanding your children to better themselves, or are you an example of a fulfilled and satisfied life?

Communication takes many forms. Whether it is in the classroom, in the kitchen, across the cell-phone airwaves, or through the mini-microphones of sophisticated satellites, it is important to ask: What is the message you are sending? Is the message understandable? What feeling do you want to express? Can you accomplish this through an e-mail? Or, do you send a letter? Should you telephone? Or, make a date to talk face-to-face? Paraverbal and nonverbal communications are so important to your message. Eye-to-eye, face-to-face, with smiles or encouraging and open palms offer a cordial greeting—here is how you can express the true feeling that you want to communicate. This is the most important kind of communication. This is when we can close the communication, not with a period at the end of a sentence on a piece of paper, but with a warm handshake or even a sincere hug.

My daughter in Colorado called her mother and said, "Mom, you should get a computer and get on e-mail! You must!"

Her mother answered, "But then we wouldn't talk so much on the phone!"

"Exactly, but we'd save dollars for sure," Carol answered.

"But I'd miss the sound of your voice. I'd miss feeling your joy, or your concern, all of which I can hear and feel in your tone and temper when you are talking. How fast or slow you talk, the hesitancy or the confident pace of your outbursts—oh, Carol, e-mail cannot come close to the telephone in communicating not just your words and a message but your mood. That's all-important. When I hear your voice—happy or sad—I feel I'm in touch with your heart!" Carol's mom concluded.

It has often been pointed out that communication is made up of four elements: substance, style, strategy, and spirit. And I declare that spirit always has the last word. Spirit may contradict or complement, but it certainly always overrides substance, style, or strategy. Effective communication may start in the head as we think through the substance and style of what we want to communicate and our strategy for doing so. But it is the spirit that communicates on the emotional level.

Dean Rusk was secretary of state during the Kennedy and Johnson administrations. Global tensions called for high-level meetings between our government and other leading governments. The Cold War was very real. When Rusk's plane landed in Washington from a European conference and he walked down the steps to meet the press, the first reporter shoved a microphone in his face and shouted, "What are the chances for peace, Mr. Secretary?" The world waited and listened. After a strong, silent pause, I heard Rusk answer, "It all depends on whether man is a rational or emotional creature."

I had just graduated and earned my academic degrees, so I intellectually scoffed at his answer, thinking to myself, *How foolish! We all know man is a rational creature.* But after more than forty years of study and practice, I have come to another position. The subconscious, I now believe, is ahead of the conscious. Yes, the head may lead the way, opening the negotiations. The brilliant brain has an unlimited ability to rationalize any position, but the spirit will have the last word. Human beings are first and last emotional creatures.

When people sincerely seek to implant the spirit of love in the core of their spirit, they find their personalities changing for the better. They look for ways to help others. They come to respect all people: even adversaries are treated with dignity. The climate for truly successful communication will be set when the objective is to build the other person's self-esteem.

The husband and wife were growing further apart. Frustrated, he said to her, "What do you expect from me! What more can I do?"

She stopped short, looked him in the eye, and softly answered, "Communicate. Just communicate with me as clearly as you do with our dog." Shocked, he waited. She went on. "Every night when you come home, the first thing you do when you come through the door is bend down, look at Poochie, and say, 'Poochie, how are you? Did you have a good day today?' Then you pat her head and rub her ears. I need to have you notice me too. I want that kind of attention. A *look,* when I'm wearing your favorite dress and a new hairdo. A *word:* 'Honey, what kind of day did you have?' And a *touch*—

give me a hug or a kiss on the cheek—a *look,* a *word,* a *touch,* is that too much to ask?"

The human family longs to be connected to one another. Make communication a high priority in life's everyday happenings.

And what about life's most important connection? How is your connection with God? No connection? A little, only when in trouble? Or is it a daily requirement for you? God's communication system far surpasses that of the one little computer chip we use to connect with each other. Then, "Why is it," I asked Mother Teresa, "that people don't rush to connect with a God who loves them so much?" In one swift, blunt word, she answered, "Distractions."

Wow! Distractions must not interfere with life's most essential connection, prayer—our communication with God— or we will lose the network that promises success.

"Call upon me, and I will show you great and wonderful things which you do not know" (Jeremiah 33:3).

That's God's way to keep you excited about tomorrow!

∽

NINE

The Contradictions—
Compromise Them
Creatively

*Where conflicting opinions share a basic truth,
you face a creative contradiction.*

Never walk away from tomorrow's dreams just because you encounter contradictions. Life is filled with contradictions. For example, in society we are all free but we are all living under law. Involved but lonely. Connected but alienated. Together but divided. Fruitful but unfulfilled. Successful but unsatisfied. Given all those social contradictions, no wonder we're confused, tense, and uptight!

Is it any wonder that contradictory orders confuse us? We're told to "take it easy" but also "get with it!" To "be serious" but also "relax!" To "have fun" but also "be good!" To "take a chance" but also "take care!" We're asked, "When are you going to make up your mind?" as often as we're advised, "Don't rush into it!"

Even our cliches are contradictory. "Strike while the iron is hot;" "Haste makes waste;" "The early bird gets the worm;" and "Fools rush in where angels fear to tread."

Contradictions—we see them in clothing fashions (clashing colors), in food (sweet and sour), and in music (minors and majors, point and counterpoint). In architecture we have strong but not heavy (soft carpet wrapped around exposed concrete). In physics we learn a basic law of contradiction (for every motion, there is an opposing motion). In religion we have the Bible (Old Testament and New Testament) and the life of Jesus (divine and human).

There are also contradictions in international politics. Different countries have different ideologies, yet we all have to share this same globe, so we must work out these contradictions creatively.

Contradictions also play a major role in social development. They mold politics, policies, economies, and business.

Here is another contradiction. You prepare for peace by being prepared for war. The people who want peace more than anyone else are the professional soldiers. A contradiction? Yes. The truth is that all of life is filled with contradictions.

Then there arc also these contradictions within you: body and spirit; thinking person and emotional person.

We cannot deny contradictions, and to ignore them may be the worst thing we can do. Instead, we need to recognize, identify, define, and deal with them. Learn to welcome life's contradictions as places where you need to make corrections. We become creative when we face a contradiction with possibility thinking.

Examine the contradictions in history—how they brought us to where we are. Some nationalities, yearning for freedom, threw out the law. The result was chaos, plundering, killing. Then, yearning for order, they brought in a new ruling party just as repressive as the last. And so we've seen throughout the world, throughout the centuries—nations going from monarchy to anarchy to dictatorship to coups, and on and on.

Contradictions will never go away. Where they take us in the future depends on how we deal with them.

Begin by looking at the contradictions in your life. Be honest with yourself as you look for them. Be like the British statesman who went to have his portrait painted. The artist said, "We'll turn you so that we can paint the left side of your face. I think it's your best profile, and the wart won't show."

But the British statesman said, "Paint me head-on, left and right, cheek, wart, and all."

Facing your contradictions means not ignoring them. To simply dismiss inner contradictions is a form of denial. Seldom is this a wise reaction. When we feel the contradictions inside us, it is time to confront them. In the process, we may uncover a subconscious cause of inner conflict or disharmony. Take, for example, the contradiction between the need for security and the need for excitement. We want to do something great, but we are afraid we will fail.

In Birmingham, Alabama, they tell the story about an important football game in which the teams were completely lopsided—one was made up of little guys and the other of big guys. It was a scary game for the little guys. As you might guess, they were losing, but miraculously by only one touchdown. With just a few minutes to go, the coach called his last time-out and brought them all together. He said, "Look, we can win this game. We're little, but Calhoun can run faster than anybody. Give the ball to Calhoun."

Back on the field, it was time for the first play. Calhoun did not get the ball. The coach, on the sidelines, kicked the turf and yelled at his quarterback. On play two, Calhoun still didn't get the ball. On the third, he still didn't get the ball. The game ended. They lost. The coach said, "Why didn't you give the ball to Calhoun?"

The quarterback said, "Calhoun wouldn't take the ball!"

Are you like Calhoun? Do you look at the big guys and decide to play it safe? Do you ignore the big contradictions and limp along, hoping that they won't hurt you if you leave them alone?

Don't resist contradictions. People who resist contradictions run away from exciting possibilities. It may be the possibility of encountering a phenomenal spiritual experience. Be brave. Face your contradictions head-on.

Don't resent contradictions. People who resent contradictions become very, very narrow. They resent anyone who has an opinion other than their own. It has to be their way! Consequently, they don't have open personalities. They clam up. They build relationships only with people who share their viewpoints. Do you know what happens in the process? They stop growing.

People this narrow and isolated become judgmental, and the only question they ask of others is, "Do they agree with my viewpoints?" Instead, they should be asking, "Are they right, or are they wrong?" and "Would what they say help me or hurt me?"

So how do we resolve life's many contradictions? Sometimes we need to convert others to our side, but most times we can compromise our contradictions creatively.

The contradiction between faith and science continues to be compromised creatively by many theologians and scientists. T. George Harris wrote in the May 1984 issue of *American Health* magazine:

Today, in medical centers and churches across the land, a new compromise is being hammered out. It's very different from the cease-fires that used to be negotiated in the old religion vs. science wars. Instead of splitting up the sufferer to let the preacher work on the spirit, the doctor on the body and the psychologist on the psyche, there's a humble effort to join forces to help a patient in any way possible.

We imagine that scientists carefully work out their equations, their calculations, their theories on paper and in the lab. Their discoveries are always the result of careful research—right? Wrong. Many of the greatest discoveries have been by fate or faith if you will.

Penicillin was discovered by an accident. And even the unraveling of the DNA mystery began by accident. S. E. Luria, the eminent molecular biologist and 1969 Nobel Laureate in medicine, confessed in his book *A Slot Machine, a Broken Test Tube* (Harper & Row, 1984) how the discovery took place. "While fighting boredom at a faculty party, Luria devised the definitive experiment to prove that bacteria mutate spontaneously. Making fun of a colleague who was pumping coins into a slot machine, it occurred to him that the mathematical principles involved in the machine's operation might be applied to his experiment with bacteria. He discovered the enzymes that splice DNA after he broke a test tube containing one bacterium and borrowed another that contained a culture of another bacterium."

Compromise creatively the scientific process. Even scientists have to have faith at some point—the faith that protons, neutrons, and electrons do indeed exist. They have to have faith that the equations indeed add up.

• • •

So how do you deal with contradictions?

The possibility thinker believes that the contradiction can be dealt with in a creatively compromising manner. Compromise calls for balancing viewpoints—for giving and taking, living and letting live, and learning from those who hold competing positions or conflicting values.

People who refuse to compromise soon find themselves living with hardened positions, iron wills, and frozen viewpoints, thereby producing only sickness within themselves. Parents and leaders in business and government are challanged daily in this art of creative compromise. For instance, in resolving conflict, they must recognize the difference between a warning and a threat. A threat is an intent to manipulate your viewpoint, whereas a warning is a sincere attempt to protect your child, your employee, or business partner from danger ahead. We need to learn the healing quality of wise compromise.

Distinguish between the positive and the negative meaning of the word *compromise*. There is such a thing as a negative compromise. Never compromise your ideals, your morals, your principles, your integrity, and your ethics. Then, indeed, *compromise* becomes a negative word. But positive compromise is something else. There is no rising up the ladder intellectually, emotionally, socially, or professionally without discovering the power of positive compromising.

I learned to compromise when I faced a contradiction. I was stuck in a rut; I had already made up my mind. Then the revelation—that is, the creative insight—appeared. It came in the form of a bright idea that taught me how to change my mind and break free of ego-directed inflexibility. The idea was, *"People who never change their minds are either perfect or stubborn."* I know I'm not perfect. And I don't want to be stubborn. So my ego was redeemed and I was liberated to see and hear the alternative and controversial opinions, viewpoints, and interpretations.

We move from emotional immaturity to emotional maturity when we are willing to amend or compromise some of our narrow ideas and hardened opinions.

Albert Schweitzer built a hospital in the jungle. One day he asked one of the natives to carry some wood. The native had been learning to read and write and replied, "I'd like to, sir, but it's beneath my dignity. I am a scholar—an intellectual."

Albert Schweitzer chuckled and said, "I've always wanted to be an intellectual too but never quite made it, so I'll carry the wood!" And he went out and carried the wood.

If you want to learn and grow, you have to admit that you don't have all the correct answers. If you want to succeed, you have to listen to the problems and criticisms that others have of your ideas.

I have a friend who claims that the complaint department is the quality control department. That is one of the principles I have learned to live by: *I don't want my own way; I want to be successful!* And another: *I don't want my own way; I want to do the right thing.* Positive compromise is being willing to humble yourself. That leads to genuine integrity of character.

Positive compromise swallows a lot of pride and absorbs a

lot of hurt. Positive compromise is lowering yourself to listen to people who are smarter than you. No matter what the subject, there are people smarter than you, and you can learn from them.

Positive compromise looks beyond the present moment to the big picture. In times of a tension in your marriage or a relationship, or between you and your associates, practice positive compromise by looking at the big picture. Do as Lincoln did. At the height of the Civil War he and his secretary of war visited the battlefield where General George McClellan was in command. They waited outside the office of McClellan for the general to return from the front lines. Finally the front door opened, and in walked the general. He saw the president and the secretary of war but never acknowledged them. Instead, he walked by them to his office. They assumed he would be back soon, so they continued to wait. When he did not appear, they sent the maid to inquire. She returned and said, "I'm sorry, Mr. President, but the general asked me to tell you that he is tired and has gone to bed." The secretary of war was shocked and said, "Mr. President, that is unacceptable; you must relieve him of command." Lincoln thought about it for a minute and said, "No, I will not relieve him; that man wins battles. I would hold his horse and wash the dirt from his boots if he could shorten this bloodshed by one hour."

Positive compromise is learning to let go. Letting go is a powerful universal principle in creative compromising. Instead of saying no, try letting go—completely! Or even partially. Let go for good, or for now. *"Learn to blend and bend to avoid a painful end."* Engineers in architecture use this principle in designing structures to survive wind pressures. Letting go can be powerfully effective. This may mean going in a new direction, revising strategy, or timing, or territory.

Compromise when you must, but don't throw away tomorrow. The old line is still true: *Let go and let God!* Learn to let go of the negative feelings, even though you have been treated rudely. Let go of the resentment, let go of the jealousy, let go of the greed, bitterness, fear, hatred, and hurt!

Learn to let go by thinking further ahead or thinking bigger. Each Easter our whole family comes home to Grandma and Grandpa's house for breakfast and our annual Easter egg hunt. We watch all of the grandchildren fill their baskets with the candy eggs. Some are chocolate, wrapped in silver foil.

One of the grandchildren, little David, is really something else. I don't know how a little guy, two years old, can explore our entire property, including all of the rooms, all of the drawers, and all of the closets. After five minutes you'd swear a tornado had just come through the place. And he leaves his sticky fingerprints everywhere. That's David.

We put everything out of reach when the grandchildren come, but there was the time Mrs. Schuller forgot to put up a little Haviland china pitcher that I had bought for her two years earlier in Germany. When I looked in the room, guess what I saw? Little David was holding that tiny pitcher, and he was standing by our fireplace, directly over the brick hearth, grinning from ear to ear.

I said, "David, give that to me. Please give that to Grandpa."

He just grinned and held on. I took hold of it and said, "Give it to me!"

He grinned but would not let go. Then I found out that he didn't have hold of it—it had hold of him. His hand was stuck inside the delicate china pitcher.

We had a real crisis. And it wasn't his hand I was worried about, it was the pitcher!

I called his father and his uncle. We had a family conference. Finally we pushed his hand farther in to see how much space there was. When we did, we could see that he had clenched his little fist tightly around his silver Easter egg inside the pitcher, and he wasn't about to let go!

I said, "Let go of the egg, David."

He just grinned.

"Let go of the egg, David."

He wouldn't let go. We pulled his hand but couldn't move it.

Suddenly I got an idea. I picked up a larger egg and said, "How would you like this big egg, David?" And he let go—and his hand came out as he grabbed the larger egg!

What negative attitude do you need to let go of today? Don't throw away tomorrow! Let go and grab hold of a bigger and better idea God has planned for you.

Perhaps the only way to deal with contradictions is to combine them creatively and produce something new. That's ingenious compromise.

I remember the time I went to Hawaii to give a lecture and spend a few days at rest. Each morning my wife and I would go for a jog in the beautiful Hawaiian paradise.

We happened to be there at the time of the annual Honolulu Open golf tournament. When we left the hotel, it was about 7 A.M. Already many, many people were lined up along the roads, waiting for the tournament.

As my wife and I jogged along, we passed two little girls, maybe eight or nine years old, who were busy by a folding table, where they had an aluminum coffeepot with a long drop cord that disappeared through an open window of a neighboring house. They also had a big pitcher of lemonade.

They were calling out to everyone coming by, "Hot steaming coffee—only twenty-five cents a cup. Fresh lemonade—only twenty-five cents a cup."

Over and over they repeated their call. My wife and I smiled as we remarked about their early morning eagerness and wondered how long it would be before they got tired and quit.

We continued jogging for the next three and a half miles, and then we turned around to jog slowly back. It took us a pretty long time to jog our seven miles.

When we were nearing the golf course again, we heard in the distance, "Hot steaming coffee—only twenty-five cents a cup. Fresh lemonade—only twenty-five cents a cup."

I said to my wife, "Boy, will their voices never get tired? I would be hoarse by this time."

Just as we approached their table, I saw them whispering,

giggling, and playing with their dolls. But I also heard their call for coffee and lemonade. What a contradiction: whispering, playing with dolls, and giggling while tending to a budding new business.

When we reached them, I noticed what they had done while we were on the road. There on the table was a cassette recorder. They had recorded their announcement!

Now that is ingenuity! We all have ingenuity, and the exciting thing is that we usually find it when we least expect it. When we are most confused, confounded, and troubled by contradictions, then we are forced to dig deeper into ourselves than ever before. And when that happens, we tap into our ingenuity.

How can we handle the contradictions that we can't handle?

God will handle the contradictions that we can't handle. God's responsibility is to step in when we have to step out. Remember, there is a good God in an evil world; there is a God of mercy when tragedies happen.

Czeslaw Milosz, the Nobel Prize–winning poet, gained international acclaim by confronting the great spiritual and political struggles in postwar Europe.

He was one of the most widely respected thinkers of the last half century. Milosz was the model of the prolific writer engaged in reconciling the major questions of his time.

He survived the Nazi occupation during World War II and the Soviet takeover that followed. As a practicing Roman

Catholic, Milosz was drawn to the Bible's Book of Job, where suffering tests a man's faith in God but does not break it. He had a profound understanding of the history of religion and the Christian church. One of the questions he was always asking is, "How could a just and good God have created a world so filled with cruelty and torture?"

Milosz credited the French wartime philosopher Simone Weil for teaching him to live with the inherent contradictions. Milosz gave this rationale for the existence of God: "It's not up to me to know anything about Heaven or Hell. But in this world there is too much ugliness and horror. So there must be, somewhere, goodness and truth. And that means somewhere God must be" (*Honolulu Advertiser,* Sunday, August 15, 2004).

By bravely accepting the reality of horrific contradictions, he avoided denial and faced truth.

Some contradictions we can't handle alone. Sometimes tragedies and sorrows come that are seemingly overwhelming.

Our family has had its share of tragedy, but we have learned through it all that there is a light behind every shadow. And when the shadow falls across your path, your mind, your mood, or your faith, remember this: the shadow is proof that there's a sun. *There can be no shadows unless there is a sun.* Trust God!

In order to deal with the contradictions between the goodness of God and the tragedy of human existence, we simply have to trust God. And if we are to trust God, we need to believe that God knows a lot more about what's going on than we do. He sees the whole picture while we see just a fraction of it. God has a perfect view; I don't. God's perspective is perfect; mine is not. When contradictions challenge our values, our belief system, and our commitments, I let go and let God handle it!

Contradictions also challenge us in daily living. We must learn to deal positively with them and find creative possibilities.

I'll never forget the story of the janitor who was sulking because he had a big mess to clean up. But that mess proved to be the best thing that ever happened to Murray Spangler.

Spangler desperately needed the janitor job, but he hated to have to scoop up all those tiny dust particles. Suddenly an idea came to him: suction. If he could suck up all those tiny particles somehow, his job would be so much easier.

The result? Murray Spangler invented the Hoover vacuum cleaner. Murray confronted his contradiction with possibility thinking. His greatest success came through his greatest annoyance.

Another contradiction is the one between the need for security and the hope for success. Everybody needs to feel secure, but at the same time, we need to feel that we're a success.

Take a boxer, for example. The boxer is very secure when he is sitting on a stool in the corner. And the baseball pitcher feels secure sitting in the dugout. But no boxer ever succeeded sitting in the corner, and it is impossible to succeed as a pitcher if you stay in the dugout.

You could put your savings in a safety deposit box, but no money ever earned interest sitting in a safety deposit box. As soon as you invest money, however, you run the risk of failure, of losing that money. So there is a contradiction. How do you resolve this?

Here's God's solution to the contradiction between security and success. First of all, God gets us out of a corner. Then He puts us in a position where success is possible—but failure is also possible. Why does He allow failure to be a possibility? Why this contradiction? Because He wants to make us into real persons, so He leads us into contradictions where faith is the only option. God wants us to learn to live by faith. And we are not living by faith or in faith until and unless we are facing the possibility of failure.

Philippians 2:13 says, "It is God at work within you giving you the will and the power to achieve His purpose."

God gives you and me a dream. God uses this dream to combine the contradictions of security and success creatively. The dream becomes a magnet that pulls us out of the security of the corner. The dream forces us to respond, and our response requires courage. It takes courage to leave the corner, to strive to succeed, to be willing to fail. In the process, the contradictions are combined creatively in a new achievement that glorifies God.

I read an interesting interview with Ross Perot in which he said, "Somebody once asked me, 'Why do you succeed?' My answer was simple: 'I only hire winners!' They said, 'Well, what if you can't find a winner?' My answer was, 'Then I hire people who hate to lose.'"

Nobody who competes can ever be a total loser because the total loser is the one who didn't dare to try. Taking a chance means you run the risk of failure. Every competitor is a winner because every competitor has shown courage.

"What a waste!" said a political candidate who lost the election.

"I don't know why I even entered," said a beauty contestant—she was "only" second runner-up out of fifty-two.

A young Olympic contender who failed to make the team exclaimed, "I'm washed up!"

"I'm finished!" moaned a businessman who had just declared bankruptcy.

"I'm a total failure. My marriage fell apart after only three years."

Wait a minute! These people may not have succeeded in their dream, but they are not total failures! All of them dared to try.

Win or lose, each is a success. And succeed or fail, each must choose not to throw away tomorrow.

Courage isn't a gift! Courage is a decision. Courage is not the absence of fear but the determination to do what you must do. Courage is spelled "INTEGRITY."

Where do you find this courage? You'll find courage when you learn from personal experience that, win or lose, you succeed merely by staying in the game.

But here is another contradiction: you will never be a total success! Neither will I, because when I choose to succeed in one area, I have accepted failure in another.

I succeeded at writing books because I chose to fail at golf. I decided that I would not spend the time trying to be a good golfer, but become a good writer. That decision was the right one for me.

The price of success is allowing yourself to fail in some other area.

So it's easy to succeed—if you choose your failures wisely.

Never give up the faith that can resolve the contradictions between the real and the ideal. I'll always remember the first time I saw the Broadway production of *The Man of La Mancha*. As many of you know, Don Quixote is the man who utters the lines, "Who's mad, the man who sees life as it is, or the man who sees life as it can be?" Then he sings, "To dream the impossible dream . . ."

Do you have trouble hoping?

Do you have trouble believing?

There's probably a contradiction between how you perceive God and how you'd *like* Him to be.

I'll never forget Brian, a young student who had dropped out of the university. When I asked him if he believed in God, he answered, "I wouldn't put money on it. But I'd like to believe that He's there."

He went on to explain that his little sister had died when

she was seven. He was only a boy himself when she died, and he was profoundly influenced by her death.

On the one hand, he couldn't believe in a God who could take his sister away from him. On the other hand, he wanted desperately for there to be a God and a heaven. He wanted the assurance that his sister was in Good Hands.

Brian didn't know how to deal with the contradictions in his belief system. The confusion resulted in an aimless life. He needed direction. He needed to resolve the ultimate contradiction in his life. When he did, the problems in his relationships cleared up. He was able to love again. He was able to hope again. He was able to believe in God.

And he was able to believe in himself again.

When you think about it, the ultimate contradiction is life and death. I agree with Sigmund Freud who said, "There is within all of us the will to live and the will to die." And until you resolve this contradiction, you will never be free to resolve any of the others. All of the contradictions we've discussed will remain a problem until you can come to terms with this central contradiction.

Maybe you're sick. Perhaps you have a terminal illness. (I prefer the term *transitional*.) Or perhaps someone close to you is near death. Then let me ask you: What makes death so hard to handle?

Death is hard to handle because it is a contradiction. Death contradicts life.

Dying is an ending, but it is also a beginning, for *every end is a new beginning.* That's the contradiction.

When you were born, it was the ending of your life in the womb and the beginning of a new life. When you stopped being a child, it was the beginning of becoming an adult. When you graduated, it was the end of your school days and the beginning of your workdays. And if you've been laid off, are unemployed, or have just retired, that's the ending of one stage of life but the beginning of something new and exciting.

When you keep that in mind, you realize that if you maintain a positive attitude toward every ending experience, you can turn every ending into a beautiful beginning. When you get married, that is the end of being single and the beginning of being a couple. And when, through death or divorce, the marriage is terminated, that ending is a new beginning.

People say this is the land of the living, but this is the land of the dying. As soon as you are born, the countdown begins. Ultimately, we all leave the land of the dying and go to the land of the living. How do I handle the ultimate contradiction between life and death? I put my trust in one person, Jesus Christ, who combines this ultimate contradiction through His resurrection.

Jesus is in the land of the living—heaven.

Every one of us can think of somebody very precious to us who has left the land of the dying and is now in the land of the living. You and I haven't taken that journey yet.

We have a living God in a dying world, preparing to take us into the land of the living. Now that's a creative resolution to life's ultimate contradiction.

Jesus focused right in on the ultimate fabulous contradiction: "If you believe in Me, you will live when you die." What a powerful paradox!

Jesus said, "I am the resurrection and the life. Those who believe in Me, though they may die, yet shall they live" (John 11:25).

That kind of faith never throws away tomorrow!

TEN

∽

Assumptions—
Let Them Lead You

All of life's decisions involve assumptions.
Learn to challenge tomorrow's negative assumptions and
explore tomorrow's positive assumptions.

As you face tomorrow, be prepared to make your most important decisions based on unprovable assumptions. We live in a universe driven by assumptions. Virtually every decision we make includes assumptions, known or unknown, conscious or unconscious, constructive or destructive, positive or negative.

We assume that the chair we sit on is strong enough to hold us. We assume that the food set before us is safe to eat. We assume that the air we breathe is nontoxic and that the hand we shake is free of disease-spreading germs. More than we are aware, our opinions, judgments, decisions, interpretations, perceptions, conclusions, and resolution of conflicts are all based on assumptions.

My friend the late Dr. George Dantzig, famed head of the math department at the University of California at Berkeley, taught me that even in solving mathematical problems, we operate more than we realize from assumptions. Dr. Dantzig learned that wise lesson in his final senior class examination. "The Great Depression was on in America in the late twenties and early thirties. We knew that when we would graduate in a few weeks, none of us would find work. We would have to join free soup lines to eat. Then our professor said, 'We will need to hire an assistant to replace my assistant who had to retire. Study hard for the final. I'll hire the one who gets the best grade.' I worked so hard to prepare for that final that I came to class late. Everyone was working on the test. I grabbed the test paper from the desk, and I solved all eight questions on the test paper but failed to solve the two problems that my professor had put on the blackboard. Because I arrived late for class I didn't hear the professor announce: 'You will be graded on the eight problems on your paper, but as you graduate, stay with the challenge of math. To challenge you all your life, I'll put on the board the two famous unsolvable problems. Even Einstein was never able to solve them!'

"Because I arrived late and didn't hear that, I was not programmed with the negative assumption that these were 'unsolvable problems.' I had solved the eight problems on the test paper, but had not solved the two problems on the board when the bell rang. I was driven by a positive assumption that some of my classmates would solve the two problems on the board so maybe I could too. So I asked the professor for more time to finish my test. 'Sure, George,' he answered. 'But put your test paper on my desk by Friday noon.' Positive that someone would solve those two problems, I desperately wanted to be that person. I worked and worked two days and nights, and I solved one! The other I never did. I turned my paper in—laid it on the professor's desk—and left depressed because I failed to solve the one problem. Sunday morning I was awakened by a loud pounding on my door. It was my professor. He was ecstatic. 'George, you made mathematics history. You made mathematics history!' 'What do you mean?' I asked. 'Well, remember you came to class late so you didn't hear my announcement about the two classical unsolvable problems? I put them on the board. George, you solved one. You didn't know they were unsolvable! You solved an unsolvable problem! Tomorrow you will be hired by this university as my assistant.'" Then George proudly added, "And I've been at Berkeley ever since."

The power of assumptions—negative or positive!

What are assumptions? They are mental observations presumed to be facts before they can be proven to be absolute reality. To make an assumption is to accept something as the truth before all sources can be traced and verified. It is committing to a viewpoint before all questions can be answered beyond a shadow of a doubt. If we were to observe and recognize all the assumptions that we make in our private, public, social, and philosophical behavior, our limited and fragile systems would collapse under the emotional and mental overload.

Learn to recognize the difference between negative and positive assumptions. Quite simply, a negative assumption is an opinion that aborts, restricts, or rejects a potentially positive mission by surrendering judgment to unproven negative presumptions. A positive assumption enhances a mission by assuming that the negative facts may be disproved as exaggerated or nonexistent, then eliminated, or rendered impotent while the positive potential may be actualized.

To live a life filled with meaning and purpose, nothing is more important than learning to manage our positive and negative assumptions. Challenge the assumptions that block you, and expose and explore the assumptions that can advance your mission goal. Don't allow negative assumptions to impetuously and impertinently destroy your dream. Affirm and explore your positive assumptions to help achieve your mission.

Challenge the negative assumptions wisely; explore the positive assumptions seriously.

Recently I returned from an enjoyable visit with my good friends Dr. Beurt SerVaas and his wonderful wife, Dr. Cory SerVaas. I really admire them both. Cory has an uncanny ability to make decisions based on positive rather than negative assumptions. At the age of fifty, married, with five children, and needing a new goal, she found a new mission: she dreamed of becoming a medical doctor and giving away her medical services for free.

She challenged the obvious negative assumptions: "You're

too old," "You can't get into medical school," "You've been out of school too long to handle the pressure," "You'll be neglecting your family and husband." Instead, she explored the positive assumptions: "If I get through med school, I can give my services away for free," "I can be a leader in the women's health movement," "I can publish my work to inform and educate women."

Not only did Cory complete her studies, become a physician, and give her medical services away for free, but she kept rising to new challenges. She regularly submitted columns to the daily newspaper, only to have them rejected. Again and again she faced negative assumptions: the editor assumed that readers would not be interested and would not take medical advice from a woman.

Committed to her dream, Cory took a bold step and purchased the historic, but bankrupt, *Saturday Evening Post*. There she created her own medical column, and reported on health-advancing discoveries. She became a forerunner in the advancement of women's health issues and one of the first advocates for nutritional supplements.

Cory saw the possibilities in life, she challenged the negative assumptions that would have defeated her dreams, and she affirmed and explored the positive assumption that she could pursue her mission and change her world.

One of the major reasons to challenge our assumptions is that the world is constantly changing and making new advances.

Many of yesterday's impossibilities are possible today. Many "facts" from yesterday are being challenged and questioned today. I have lived long enough to see "scientific truths" in my younger years being disproved by the latest research. Professors in the leading universities in every department again and again proclaim "facts" that are later disproved by some researcher who observed that these so-called facts were based on assumptions that were unproved. Progress often happens when underlings challenge the assumptions of their superiors.

I just received a copy of a biography by Bob Burke and Barry Epperson, *W. French Anderson: Father of Gene Therapy* (2003), for which I was honored to write the foreword. Dr. Anderson, known as "French," tells a fascinating true story. In his own words, he told me, "I've talked about gene therapy in human beings since I was a senior in college. It was a radical idea. In my senior year at Harvard. I was attending a graduate seminar of doctors and senior graduate students. There was a session on protein hemoglobin, the pigment in the blood. At the time, I was doing research work putting genes from one bacterium into another, changing its properties. So I raised my hand and asked, 'Why can't you do that in a human being? Why couldn't you treat sickle-cell anemia by using a gene to create normal hemoglobin?'

"The scorn and ridicule in the room was obvious: 'This is a serious scientific meeting; don't be silly, don't bring up science fiction.' So I hid off in a corner, and when the meeting was over I was going to sneak out so that nobody saw me. But one professor, John T. Edsall, one of the great names in science, came up to me, patted me on the shoulder, and said, 'Interesting idea.' That's all he said. And I thought, *If Professor Edsall thinks this is an interesting idea, I'm going to do it.*"

Today it is widely believed that gene therapy will revolutionize the practice of medicine, becoming the fourth revolution of medicine. Why? Because one man was able to pinpoint and affirm a positive assumption. One professor saw the possibility in a young man's idea. That same young graduate student continued to let his positive assumptions lead him through years of trial and error in the exploration of gene therapy: identifying the engineering code in our bodies that defines who and what we are and isolating genes and manipulating them to treat disease.

On September 14, 1990, Dr. Anderson saw the first fruits of his efforts. His four-year-old patient, Ashanthi DiSilva, received the first treatment using this genetic therapy. This young girl had a defective gene causing her to suffer from the "bubble boy syndrome." Through his breakthrough treatment, Dr. Anderson was able to give her a normal life. Today there are many patients who have been helped through his work. Gene therapy has great promise and is predicted to help many thousands of patients, but it is still in the experimental stage.

Suppose Dr. Anderson had not believed in his idea. Suppose he had listened to the negative voices and ridicule. Thank God, he listened to his professor's one positive affirming word. The medical assumptions tomorrow will be different from those of today. Today the positive assumptions are building on a humble foundation: "We don't know it all, and there is room for more discoveries."

Can we avoid making decisions based on risky assumptions by refining our judgments through scientific tests? Probably. Surely we should not be reckless and pursue risky assumptions without seeking the greatest wisdom possible. But are such tests totally free of assumptions? Are the questions, the answers, the interpretations all drawn from error-free perceptions or intuitions, or do they also derive from prejudices, preconceptions, or assumptions?

In 1959 I was preparing a large-scale development plan for our new church complex. It would be a complex and challenging assignment for any architect. Richard Neutra, already one of the world's most esteemed architects, was my choice. His face had just appeared on the cover of *Time* magazine. One day Neutra was approached by Frank Barron at the University of California at Berkeley. Barron himself was famous for creating tests to determine a person's occupational talents. Dr. Barron approached Richard Neutra and said, "Let me test you, Mr. Neutra, to see what occupation you should be pursuing." Both had a chuckle. For the fun of it, Neutra took Barron's test. The results were shocking. In architecture as a career, Neutra failed—architecture for him rated seventeenth, low on the scale. In sixteen other professions he scored higher. For what other professions was he more naturally gifted? The test pointed him to philosophy, psychology, or spiritual and religious professions. Dr. Barron was shocked and said to Neutra, "Well, don't go on being a world-famous architect!" Both laughed. "But something may be amiss in my test," Barron concluded. "Or probably the test really shows what a great architect must be—an emotionally sensitive, 'spiritual' personality."

Assumptions are inevitable. But just as the body's muscles need energy to maintain their physical fitness, so spiritual fitness and emotional wellness draw their power from faith "muscles," which are strengthened by the regular exercise they get from challenging unprovable assumptions.

So how do we make decisions—intelligently and responsibly—when assumptions are a part of the process? It is not enough to be enthusiastic. Get smart.

Research the viability of your assumptions by seeking the opinions of the most knowledgeable and most unprejudiced people. Test the veracity of your supposition in a variety of ways: focus groups, test marketing, or laboratory research.

Education is all-important. Note the difference between the traditional philosophy of education in Europe and the West and the traditional philosophy of education in Asia and the Middle East. Western education often focuses on facts, and a top student is labeled "knowledgeable." In Asia and the Middle East, education traditionally focuses on principles. A top student in this educational environment is often called not "knowledgeable" but "wise." The complex and often complicated world of today and tomorrow will require education to focus more on universal principles to guide humankind.

Can we teach wisdom, including the wisdom to manage assumptions? I think so. I had professors who intuitively taught the principles of humility and wisdom.

"I don't know all the answers, and some of my answers are wrong." What wisdom there is in such humility! It protects us from "I know it all" arrogance. It restrains us from communicating as facts what are in reality assumptions. It keeps our minds open to discover room for correction and improvement as we move toward mental reactions and responses.

One of the most esteemed architectural structures is the Kimball Art Museum in Fort Worth, Texas. A member of the major donor family gave me a private tour. She appropriately praised the famed gold-medal architect Louis I. Kahn. "His greatness was due to his humility," she said. "We were ready to let out bids. I was given the chance to meet with him and review the plans. I was so impressed." She continued, "Then I blurted out to Louis Kahn, 'Sir, I found some doorknobs that I think would be perfect here.'" She watched for his reply. "Mrs. Kimball, we are ready to begin. Every detail has been decided. And when I have all the answers, I can be sure of one thing: some of my answers are wrong. Let's see the doorknobs you found." He accepted them! That's humility.

Challenge your own assumptions with similar humility. Keep your mind open for new input and new answers. That's wisdom—the better part of education.

Learn to listen when the agenda leads to debatable interpretations or controversial decisions based on assumptions. Listen wisely. Don't argue. Ask questions. Are we educated, or are we indoctrinated? Are our teachers and preachers truly honest and humble in sharing their insights? Or are they communicating prejudices from their own biased viewpoint?

Some biased professors and religious leaders have political, religious, or antireligious prejudices, and they indoctrinate rather than educate others. A truly humble educator seeks to teach by asking wise questions that will bring light to the subject rather than by making pontifical and prejudicial pronouncements. He or she also knows that we don't know it all, that some of our answers may be wrong, or that they are no longer relevant or up-to-date given new inventions, discoveries, and fresh insights from the latest research.

We all must challenge our own positions and debate our own assumptions. Be your own devil's advocate. Remember, in real life you don't want to win a debate, you want to arrive at the right conclusion. You don't want people to agree with you if you're making a mistake. You don't want your own will or way; rather, you want to do what is right and best. Integrity and excellence are most important, and remembering that will keep your ego in place. You're on the way to cultivating mental habits that will help you move ahead with positive assumptions that can turn impossibilities into possibilities.

But negative assumptions also must be wisely studied. We cannot totally avoid the power of negative assumptions, and that may be good, for negative assumptions can be life-saving.

But adults carry a lot of negative baggage that causes prejudice and intolerance and is truly destructive.

It has long been established and observed that prejudice is not natural to children. A few hundred years ago, when every country was ruled by a monarch or a king, we're told that the children of the king would play with the children of the peasants, and all would have a wonderful time together. Children are all the same. They have to be taught prejudice.

When I visited the Museum of Tolerance in Los Angeles, I was deeply affected by it.

To enter the Museum of Tolerance, you have to choose one of two doors. Over one door is a sign reading, "I am not prejudiced." Over the other door a sign says, "I am prejudiced." The guide looked at me and asked, "Okay, Dr. Schuller, which door do you choose to go through into the exhibit?" "Oh," I said, "I think I'll have to go through the door that says, 'I'm prejudiced.'" He raised his eyebrows. "Are you sure? Don't you want to go through the one that says, 'I am not prejudiced?'" I told him no.

"Well, Dr. Schuller," he replied, "the truth is that everybody goes through the door that says, 'I am prejudiced.' You see, the other door does not open."

The museum planners, however, might consider making one small change: they should build one little tiny door about forty-six inches high in the big door that says, "I am not prejudiced." Little children should go through that door. Their minds haven't been polluted yet with all kinds of prejudice—

religious prejudice, political prejudice, economic prejudice, racial prejudice, or cultural prejudice.

As we learn to manage our assumptions, we must learn to recognize that certain of our positive assumptions may be God-inspired gifts. One such gift is intuition.

In the July 2003 issue of *Reader's Digest* is an article by Lisa Collier Cool entitled "Intuition: You've Got It—Here's Why You Should Use It." In her opening lines she tells this story:

In a large, crowded hospital in Zimbabwe, a 30-year-old woman was lying on a gurney about to be wheeled into the operating room for minor gynecological surgery when Rebecca Bingham, M.D., happened to walk by. Although she'd never seen the patient before—and knew nothing of her medical history—the doctor had a sudden sense of alarm. "I felt I should check her heart," says Dr. Bingham.

She put her stethoscope to the woman's chest, and heard a murmur—abnormal blood flow through the heart, a possible sign of mitral stenosis, a heart condition that can cause serious complications if the person is anesthetized. Bingham alerted the surgeons, who canceled the operation to further evaluate the patient. Tests confirmed that she did, in fact, have the dangerous condition.

An amazed surgeon asked Dr. Bingham why she had suspected the disorder. The family practitioner replied that it was "just a hunch."

Psychologists like Timothy D. Wilson, Ph.D., professor at the University of Virginia, and author of *Strangers to Ourselves,* believe such hunches are prompts from the adaptive unconscious. This is not the Freudian realm of repressed memories and primitive emotions. The adaptive unconscious is a mechanism in the brain that processes an ocean of sensory information.

Like Dr. Bingham, most of us have had remarkably accurate intuitions that seem to spring from nowhere. We call these mysterious flashes of insight hunches, gut feelings, animal instinct, ESP, or even a sixth sense. Some people dismiss them as lucky guesses.

These hidden powers of perception, says Gary Klein, Ph.D., author of *Intuition at Work,* are what allow people to "see the invisible." But Dr. Klein, a cognitive psychologist from Fairborn, Ohio, once a skeptic himself, no longer dismisses the power of intuition.

Dr. Bingham thinks that her hunches have resulted in some amazing diagnoses, including detecting lung cancer in a patient who came in for a routine physical. "Though this woman didn't have obvious symptoms, I thought I ought to check her out with a chest X ray." Bingham ordered a chest X ray, which showed a very small, still treatable tumor. "Now I tell medical students that if they ever get a feeling that something is wrong with a patient, they should listen, because it might save a life."

Yes, we must learn to listen and follow that inner voice—carefully and prayerfully.

Are our assumptions the output of intuition? Dr. Viktor Frankl and Dr. Karl Menninger were two of the greatest psychiatrists of the twentieth century. Both were friends of mine from whom I learned a lot. Both remarked independently in one of our many visits that I was a most intuitive person. Surprised, I asked each of them, "What is intuition?" They gave the same answer: "We don't really know!"

Teilhard de Chardin, one of the most respected philosopher-theologians, said, "We are not human beings. We are spiritual beings on a human journey. I believe that intuition, more than we can ever know, may be the Spirit of God guiding and leading us."

Yes, all humanity lives under assumptions. I call that living under the cosmic force of faith. The Bible defines *assumption* when and where it defines *faith:* "Faith is the evidence of things not seen" (Hebrews 11:1). Faith, then, is a mental process of assuming the reality of what cannot be proven to be true. Therefore, it is humanly impossible to avoid all assumption-based decisions in this business of living. All human beings live with assumptions, which means that everyone lives under the cosmic force of faith. I assume the sun will rise tomorrow. I assume I will be alive tomorrow. So I assume tomorrow will come to me, bringing purpose and pleasure in real positive possibilities.

Recently, I was in China, where I was asked to speak to a university student body about possibility thinking. The government of China had translated and published my book *You Can Become the Person You Want to Be* and allowed it to be distributed throughout China a few years earlier.

I delivered my lecture to an audience of bright, young, eager students. My assignment was to challenge them to believe in tomorrow's dreams. I was asked not to speak about God, but they did want to hear how to use possibility thinking in planning the future.

I wondered how this young high-tech generation would relate to the old, white-haired American. But their response to me was enthusiastic, and when the audience was dismissed, some students gathered around me to ask questions.

One young student said, "Dr. Schuller, your possibility-thinking talk is much needed for us, because our future is so uncertain. Each one of us is fearful about our careers. We are competing with each other for the same positions. But you ended your talk mentioning faith. That is so foreign to us. That does not fit in with our scientific reality thinking. What do you mean?"

I hoped my brief answer could help him understand. As he listened intently, I said, "Human beings are hardwired for faith!"

The student replied, "Why do you say we need faith in the infrastructure of human thinking?"

I answered, "We are a species uniquely created and designed. Humans are the only creatures that have a mind—to think, to reason, to imagine, to assume, to have faith. Faith to humans is what wings are to a bird. We are created with a mind to imagine—wings of imagination. We are distinctive among creatures. The human species is designed to be an intelligent, free-choosing, independent-thinking, decision-making, opinion-forming, and assumption-managing creature. But that only happens if we become possibility thinkers. I am a believer in God, and I hold to the possibility that God created us to be persons, not puppets or computerized creatures. He wanted us to be creative creatures. God could have set up human existence to make it possible for us to know, without a shadow of doubt, like we know the reality of the sun and the earth, that there is a God. But leaving ultimate reality as a mighty mystery forces us to mentally reach beyond our grasp."

The student asked, "Why are you a believer in God, Dr. Schuller, when you know you can't prove it?"

I answered, "Because my faith in God answers so many questions about life—in science, about humanity, and about religious impulses. And the rejection of this faith, in my mind, does not adequately answer these questions but, in fact, creates many more questions. It takes a lot more faith not to believe in God than to believe in God."

The student responded, "So is not 'faith in faith' enough? You say we should believe in God. Isn't it good enough to just be 'spiritual'?"

I said, "As we face this mystery of being spiritual, we dare not make a misjudgment. We need a divine revelation. Human reasoning at best is too risky.

"Religion can lead to reckless mythology or superstition, which can lead to a toxic faith.

"What we need is divine revelation. I have come to believe that if there is an intelligent and affectionate God, then He must reveal himself. To keep human beings guessing about the truth would be something a caring God could not do. God is morally obligated to expose Himself. Judaic-Christian teachers believe that God has done this in and through the lives of great people whose true stories are collected in a book called the Holy Bible—Moses, prophets, David, Jesus, and Paul.

"In the Bible, Christ Himself claims to be the ultimate revelation—God Divine in human life."

The student then asked, "What difference has faith in God made in your life?"

I responded, "I know that the kind of faith that I have chosen to shape my mind has turned me into a creative person. I can guarantee that my faith has made a marvelous difference in how I approach assumptions that are pregnant with positive possibilities! I know I'm a far more creative person because I believe in the creative God that Jesus Christ believed in. I am more successful because, as a believer in God since childhood, I grew up a possibility thinker, believing that nothing is impossible. I grew up as a faith creature programmed to grasp great positive possibilities. What a difference this kind of thinking has made in my life!"

The student probed: "But what if your decision is not the right one? How can you live with that?"

"Because I know I'm a better person because of this faith. I know that teaching others to embrace this positive thinking has helped millions of people *to believe in themselves.*"

"If I am wrong, it has been a blessed error!"

I returned to my hotel in Beijing, stimulated by these future world leaders who were curious to know more about faith and God. They didn't turn this old white-haired American off; they were earnestly looking for more than their atheistic academic world was offering.

So I asked myself, What really is faith? How do I define it? I talk about it all the time. My first sermon before the entire faculty in theological graduate school was on faith. It has been the centerpiece in my studies and sermons and thirty-five books for over fifty years. And my lifetime focus on faith has led me to study and learn from the greatest psychiatrists in the twentieth century.

Look where this theological specialty has led me. I have come to believe that *faith is a fact, not a fantasy.* Individuals who live with faith are allowing their positive assumptions to drive their lives. Faith is not a myth. It is a scientific reality operating in human personality and human behavior.

Michael Guillen, one of the most respected scientific analysts in the world today, has for years been seen for his scientific analysis on the ABC network, regularly appearing on *Good Morning America* and *20/20*. Here is his latest news report. Scientists of the highest rank are now declaring that a human being does not consist just of body and mind, as it was popular to say late last century—you'll recall all the mind-body studies that were in vogue then, and to a lesser degree still are. Rather, scientists are now beginning to recognize the existence and importance to our overall health of "spirit." In other words, medical science's view of human beings has gone from being purely "somatic" (i.e., we're just a body), to "psychosomatic" (i.e., we're body and mind), to now "theosomatic" (i.e., we're body, mind, and spirit). Here in the full-blown theosomatic view is where we can begin to understand how "faith power" operates. Here is the arena where we can see how "assumptions" are conceived!

All my life I have been a faith-driven human. All my decisions are made by faith. Now I see that *faith* and *assumption* describe the same mental activity. And human beings are designed and engineered by a creator to be integrated persons operating under a law of faith, which is as real as the law of gravity. Erik Erikson, father of child psychology, said that in the first stage of human life, from birth to the age of two, a child has to discover trust. As a theologian, I call that learning to believe, or acquiring a positive attitude of confidence. In short, humans must learn to believe in the unprovable. That is, we must learn to listen to the silent voice of "assumptions" that enter our spiritual nature and our human awareness. We must learn to perceive that birds were designed to do the impossible—to fly! So they were given wings. Humans were designed to achieve the impossible, so God created us with wings in our thinking system called faith. Secularists use a different word to describe the same mental activity. Instead of faith, they call it *assumption thinking*. Psychologists emerged only one hundred years ago who described the same function and called it *positive thinking*. I call it *possibility thinking*. I learned that as a follower of Jesus. It is time for us to see and declare that this mental behavior points to what is a natural reality operating in this creature called a human being.

Newton discovered gravity with the question "Why did that apple fall down, and why didn't it float away?" Humans must now discover what I call the law of faith. Psychologists and theologians must come to discover that human beings are, by nature, faith-created creatures.

Why were humans created to be faith-driven or assumption-compelled creatures? Because unless and until, at decision-making time, we learn to accept positive possible proposals that are unprovable, we will be unable to face and embrace risk. And only when we dare to make decisions that involve risks will we truly become the creative and progressive people I call possibility thinkers.

So faith is a fact, not a fantasy. And faith is a mountain-moving force, but *faith is not a value.*

Faith is a force, not a value. Faith in itself is amoral. It is not in itself religious or spiritual. It is a natural systemic channel designed in every human being to be the pipeline for creative imagination, for spiritual impulses to enter and do their work. There is no compassion or conscience in faith. Faith can be good or ill, divine or demonic, intelligent or unintelligent. It all depends on what value is allowed to be transported through the power of faith, humans to God.

Faith is a connecting power, connecting people to people, ideas to achievement, projects to possibilities.

Faith is the cell phone; that is the power. The value is in the message it delivers.

Faith is the satellite; that is the power. The value is in the programming it sends out.

Faith is the pipeline; that is the power. The value is what pours through it—water, gas, or oil.

Faith is a delivery power; the value comes in the product or human value it delivers.

Faith is the plane, the ship, train, or truck; that is the power. The value is in the cargo, not in the delivery channel.

Faith can deliver values—good or evil. We see the death and destruction caused when humans focus their faith on evil. Consider the terrorists who destroyed the New York Twin Towers. Others focus their faith on what is good. Mother

Teresa, whom I knew and loved, truly was a saint. The source and the object of her grand and glorious faith was the God whom she saw in Jesus Christ. Her faith was not a religion but a personal relationship with Jesus Christ.

Faith is a decision, not a debate. In Hope College, my debate team won forensic honors, and we were elected to the national honorary forensic society, Pi Kappa Delta. I still have the solid gold key with a ruby stone I received when I was invited to join this society.

So when I later graduated from theology school, I became a fully credentialed clergyman ready to debate the secular world. I still recall meeting and debating an intellectual atheist. I lost that private debate—big time! I have never admitted that failure until now, at the age of seventy-eight.

He hit me with this argument: "Reverend Schuller, I can never accept your position, for all your arguments are based on assumptions. All religious positions are based on assumptions. I'm a lawyer and a scientist; I build my case on facts, never on faith."

I was floored. I had no answer. I backed away—until I started writing this book. I could not die without confronting my biggest failure. Now I've faced my contradiction. Wow! What a creative experience that has been!

Today, I would welcome a debate with him—on a national platform. I would wait for him to make his summary statement: "Everything you propose, Dr. Schuller, is based on assumptions." I would smile. Pause. Step closer to meet him face-to-face. I would lock eyes. Then I would answer, "I agree with you. My religion is based on assumptions—and so is your unbelief. Let's shake hands. Both of us are living with assumptions we have freely chosen to believe and build a life on. In the Bible the word *assumption* is spelled F-A-I-T-H."

Atheism is a negative assumption in an impossibility thinker's mind.

Theism is a positive assumption in a possibility thinker's mind.

Take your choice.

As a possibility thinker, I call faith in God the highest, holiest, and most honorable and respectable practice of positive assumptions.

I've learned to live every day led by positive assumptions rather than by negative assumptions. I have had so many positive experiences that I cannot explain without believing that God is real. Faith in God is a decision. I won't debate it. So I have chosen to believe because my faith works for me in my daily living and in facing the ultimate mystery—life beyond this life.

Faith is a commitment, not an argument. Faith is a choice, based on values, so it calls for a commitment. "I might be wrong, but I'm giving my heart to my mission." "I want my life to count!" Commitment delivers awesome power to possibility thinking.

"But I'm an agnostic," a bright young man said to me, adding, "what's wrong with that?" What is wrong with that is it is not right. Neutrality is indecisive. One side or the other is right. Theism or atheism? One is right, the other wrong. Indecision is a decision that avoids and evades the call to commitment. Agnosticism is a path that leads nowhere. Commitment is the path that leads somewhere.

I'm a pragmatist; I'll choose a faith, a philosophy, a theology, a psychology if it helps me in daily living. The religious faith I've chosen has made me a dreamer of great impossible dreams, and it works wonders.

It has given me the people, friends, and energy to make these dreams come true. That is maximized living; that is real life.

If it works, I'll listen.

If it works, don't throw it away.

If it works, try it; it might save your life.

Jesus said, "I am the way, the truth and the life" (John 14:6). I assume this is spiritual reality. My life has been shaped by this positive assumption, and I would hold it even if there were serious reasons to reject it. Why? Because of the gracious and good life I've lived, inspired by the life and teachings of Jesus. I truly believe He is the answer. So I choose Jesus Christ. If I'm wrong, I'm in the best company—and I'm sure I'm on the right page! Just look how my faith has shaped all of my tomorrows.

I repeat what I said earlier: "If I'm wrong, it's been the most blessed error in my life. Amen!"

ELEVEN

Believe in Tomorrow

I cannot promise that you will change the *world, but I can
promise that you can change* your *world!*

"There is a man on the line calling from Monte Carlo,"
my secretary said. "He wants to speak with you. Will
you take the call?"

I was shocked. Of the thousands of calls I've taken the past
fifty years, this one stands out. "You mean Monte Carlo, home
of Prince Rainier?" "Yes," she answered. I had never been to
Monte Carlo, and I did not know that *Hour of Power* could be
seen there.

I picked up the phone. The caller told me his name—one
I'd never heard. "Dr. Schuller, we have never met," he said,
"but you saved my life—literally. I am alive today because of
you. You alone. I need to come to Garden Grove to see you, to
thank you."

Some days after that surprising phone call came the message, "I'm here in California at the L.A. airport." It was the

stranger from Monte Carlo. "Can I come right over?" he asked. "Of course," I answered. I offered to send my driver. "I have my own driver," he answered. "Let me put him on the line and you can give him directions."

An hour later the man arrived, and my secretary showed him in. She opened the door, and I was not prepared for what I saw. A tall, handsome, broad-shouldered man, probably in his early fifties, limped toward me, a white cane in his right hand. A black patch covered his left eye, while his right eye stared upward, unfocused. One leg was conspicuously shorter, the custom black Oxford shoe built up with a platform sole probably five inches thick. Standing beside him was his driver, who guided him gently. The driver spoke first, apologizing for showing up without a personal invitation. "As you can see, Juan here is blind. But he's alive thanks to you. I'm living in Beverly Hills. Juan and I were business partners and friends before his accident. He wants to tell you his story himself."

"Please be seated." I gestured to a corner sofa. Juan walked slowly, head held high, and sat down, guided by his driver. He placed the white cane next to him and patted it, feeling its handle carefully so he'd have no problem finding it.

"Thank you, Dr. Schuller," he said. "Thank you for agreeing to see me." I saw his face quiver. "How much time do I have, Reverend?" he asked. "All the time you want," I answered sincerely.

He spilled out his story. He was the only child of a wealthy Cuban family and had inherited the entire family fortune. He guessed correctly and early on that Fidel Castro might succeed and that every capitalist would lose all possessions. So he sold everything except his large private yacht and sailed to Monte Carlo, where he bought a luxurious estate behind iron gates on the waterfront. His two-hundred-foot luxury yacht, near Prince Rainier's yacht, was docked in front of his home. He had no secrets, confessing to me that though he had never married, he was heterosexual and very active sexually. He could afford the most beautiful and expensive women. Then one weekend he and his girlfriend left to go to Switzerland for a weekend. He chose one of his Rolls Royces, and hardly had he left the house when it started to rain. He was going too fast on a wet curve, lost control, and wrapped the car around a tree. He awakened from a coma seven months later to find out what had happened. His beautiful girlfriend had been killed instantly. He was now totally blind, and his left leg, now healed, was over five inches shorter. And, most depressing of all, his sexual powers were totally destroyed.

Several months passed. His money and his body could no longer give him pleasure. He went to bed every night hoping he would die in his sleep. He could not face his tomorrows, so he carefully began to plan his suicide. He would use one of his handheld revolvers. He would do it on his yacht on a Sunday morning at 11:00 A.M. He would dismiss his staff. Then, with no one around, he would turn his television to full volume, keeping the TV off for the moment. He would put the gun to his temple with his right hand, and with his left he would press the TV "on" button. When the whole room blasted full of whatever happened to be broadcast at the moment, he could then pull the trigger and no one would hear the shot.

He followed the suicidal scheme as he planned. Sunday morning came. He could sense he was all alone. No one to share a tomorrow with him. So he stood upright and fingered the TV volume, turning it up to full power. He touched the steel barrel to his temple. He pressed the "on" button, but before he could pull the trigger a voice bellowed forth. It was a TV preacher yelling his opening sentence: "This is the day the Lord has made; let us rejoice and be glad in it!"

As Juan recounted the story, his body rocked back and forth on the sofa, as if he were in a rocking chair. "Dr. Schuller, those words exploded through my mind and soul. It was like a divine shock therapy. I was frozen with a feeling I'd never felt before. I could not pull the trigger. I could not even hold the gun. It fell to the floor. And I dropped to the floor and listened to your every word. I spent the next week waiting for the next Sunday. Would you be back? And you were. And the next week. And you were there again. I was born again. I felt Christ's spirit coming into my life. I couldn't wait for the next Sunday.

"Then I went to my jeweler and said, 'Is there a symbol for hope in the Bible?' And he said, 'Of course, Juan, it's the anchor.' And he quoted the Bible verse 'Hope is the anchor of the soul' (Hebrews 6:19). 'Oh, that's perfect,' I said. 'Then make me an anchor with a chain designed with links to match the links of the anchor chain of my yacht. On one side of the anchor I want three initials in silver, R.H.S. That man brought new life to me.'"

Now Juan reached in his inside coat pocket and drew out a flat, slender package and handed it to me. "That's my thank-you," he said. "You saved my life!"

The package was heavy. I opened it to see the most beautiful gold anchor on an exquisite chain with links shaped like no other chain in any jewelry store. I am wearing it now as I write these words. It speaks to me silently: "Hope is the anchor of the soul."

Before Juan found God, he was shipwrecked in the sea of life, but now he was anchored to a mighty force—faith. "I know now," he said, "that there is something more to life than I had ever known, and it is beautiful."

Juan was facing his tomorrows with a new sense of inner purpose because he found an eternal hope in his soul that sustained him. His face glowed. And the glow was still there when I visited him years later as an overnight guest in his Monte Carlo home. Only a few months ago Juan passed away. He didn't change the world, but he surely changed his world.

He went from a life shipwrecked to a life anchored in hope.

I was in a restaurant recently in a distant city, and a handsome young man was our waiter. His appearance was striking; he could have been a young lawyer, clergyman, or high-powered executive. He seemed out of place waiting tables. So I asked him, "Is this your lifetime career?"

He replied, laughing, "No. I'm searching."

He recognized my face and knew that I was a pastor. He continued, "I wonder if you knew my parents. They were active in a church near you." He named the church, a wonderful Christian church, but I didn't know them.

"Do you share their faith?" I asked him.

"Well," he said, "right now I'm searching for the truth. That's why I came here, but now I'm moving to northern California—there are lots of religious and spiritual teachers there." Then he repeated, "I'm searching for the truth."

Before I finished my dinner, he brought the subject up again, and I offered, "May I give you some advice?"

"Please do," he replied. "I respect you. I listen to you often."

So I looked at the face of this bright, promising seeker, and I said, "I will soon be seventy-eight years of age. I've met many people like you, all searching for the truth. Let me tell you where that road will lead—to confusion.

"You can stop searching," I said. "Truth isn't a book. Truth is a person. His name is Jesus Christ. He said, 'I am the way, the truth, and the life. He that follows Me shall not walk in darkness but shall have the light of life.' I trust him. If we can't trust Jesus Christ, who in the world can we trust? Follow Him, and you will know truth."

This man's life was not shipwrecked but was adrift and needed to anchor in a safe harbor.

Is this young waiter still searching? I don't know. I doubt

I'll ever see or meet him again, but he seemed so lost, his life so directionless, that I'm concerned for his tomorrows. Will he find God, the Anchor of hope that Juan found?

In another city, I got on the elevator in the hotel, and there was a young, attractive, well-dressed woman. I said, "I hope you have a good day today."

She said, "I hope so too. This is my first day on the job. I'm working here in the hotel."

"Well, I make a prediction," I offered. "You're going to have a great day. Something good is going to happen to you, and it's going to be terrific." She seemed shocked but grateful as the elevator door opened and we went in different directions.

Back in my room, I had my work papers spread out over the bed and on the side table and chair. Not wanting anything touched, I hung a Do Not Disturb sign on the door. As I left for my meetings, I saw the supervisor in charge of maid service and said, "Will you see to it that nobody enters my room? I have papers out that I don't want moved." She assured me everything would be left alone.

When I returned later that afternoon, I again saw the supervisor and told her I was ready to have the room cleaned. I would now be there to watch and make sure that my work wasn't disturbed. She promptly called a maid down the hall to come in to clean. Here, in a maid's uniform, came the same young woman I had met that morning in the elevator.

"Well, how is your first day going?" I inquired as she came in.

"Pretty good," she answered quietly.

"What did you do before this job?" I asked, always curious about the people I meet.

She paused from her cleaning and looked up. "I was in a correctional institution for a few years," she confessed. "I committed six felonies."

"Wow!" I exclaimed, shocked that such an attractive young woman could ever be in prison. "Are you alone?"

"I have a seven-year-old daughter," she answered, "but I'm not married." Then she added, "I never have been."

As we continued our dialogue, I wanted so much to encourage her and give her hope. I needed to share my faith with her. She was looking for a fresh start. She needed God.

"You know," I said, "there is a God who knows you. And He loves you. There is a whole new life waiting for you out there." I don't recall all the words that came out of my heart to hers, but it was not a canned sermon. It was a sincere witness of the positive difference that faith in Jesus Christ makes. Finally, I asked her, optimistically, "May I pray for you?"

"Yes, please," she answered, the tears starting to flow down her cheeks. She was not shipwrecked like Juan, nor was she drifting like the waiter in a search for truth. She was lost in the sea of life. How dangerous and vulnerable! She needed an anchor for her soul.

So before she left I offered her a gift, a book from my briefcase—*The World's Greatest Power Thinker.* "It's about the life of Jesus Christ," I said, and she cheerfully thanked me.

Three people from different parts of the world, all three desperate in their need to find a solid faith that would anchor their lives in a hope that would make them believe in tomorrow.

In high school I had to memorize the famous poem "Invictus," by William Ernest Henley.

Out of the night that covers me.
Black as the Pit from pole to pole,
I thank whatever gods may be
For my unconquerable soul.
. . . .
I am the master of my fate:
I am the captain of my soul.

In high school I recited these words, but without any enthusiastic conviction, for my faith was already anchored strong with a higher power. My testimony was—and still is—that Christ is the master of my fate; Christ is the captain of my soul!

With all of life's personal and professional conflicts, it's easy to lose our way in our journey of life. We need a higher power who has the larger perspective.

All of life is so very complex, and we do not have all the answers. We need a God to keep us on the right track and correct us when we make mistakes, to guide us when we are not sure which path to choose.

So, what type of higher power do you and I need? Not just one who instills wisdom, but one who builds character. I have come up with my own qualifications for the kind of higher power I need. My God must be able to fulfill these needs:

He must be a kind and loving personal God who radiates goodness, and He must also be an honest and honorable God.

He must be a God I can trust to design the strategy in my life so that under His careful watch I will become a better, wiser, more beautiful person, changing my world and having hope for tomorrow.

He must be a positive God who keeps me believing in my dreams through any and all hurts, interruptions, disastrous setbacks, grief or guilt, failure or defeat, to renew me and help me keep on keeping on.

I need a mighty God to supply me with the resources that will see me through to success.

I need a God who will not fail me as my leader, guide, and the captain of my soul. He must inspire, shape, and support my life's dream to serve humanity.

I need a God who believes in me.

Where can I find that kind of a God? I found that kind of a God in the Holy Bible and in Jesus Christ. What kind of a life has that faith delivered? A life that is anchored with hope and filled with love. To summarize, this faith gives:

A purpose to live for.

A self that you can live with.

A faith that you can live by.

A leader you can trust.

A love that will save you.

Derek Fisher is a name that most basketball fans know. As a point guard for the Los Angeles Lakers, Derek helped his team win three straight NBA titles. He set or tied career highs in eleven categories, including scoring twenty-eight points against the Chicago Bulls. But what is most impressive is that Derek is known for his moral stature both on and off the court. Recently he came to the Crystal Cathedral to share why his faith in God gives him not only daily guidance but also a greater purpose in life.

"It's important to live by faith," he said. "God has a plan for all of us. I was chosen to walk the path of playing in the NBA. God's plan for me is a calling to go out, compete, and play hard in the name of God.

"I'm thankful for the position I'm in and the family I had to support me and encourage me all through my career."

Derek's career and calling didn't always seem so clear. As an avid math student in high school, Derek figured his life's work would include accounting. His high school basketball career, though not astounding, did reward him with a scholarship to a small college in his hometown of Little Rock,

Arkansas. But according to Derek, God had a plan for Derek's life.

"It just proves that God has a plan for you. No matter what school you go to, where you live, what color you are, how much money your family has, or what kind of a house you live in, God's plan will see you through."

When the NBA and Lakers called Derek, his career was on the way, big time, and he had a new mission. He could now share his faith and encourage young people, helping them to believe in exciting tomorrows.

Derek excitedly talked about his special ministry to children. "I tell the children that it's extremely important to believe in yourself and in the life God has for you. A lot of times young people feel alone. It's important for them to realize God specifically places people in their lives for a reason. When Mom and Dad are getting on you, remember, God puts your parents in your life, and your grandparents and other relatives. They're there for you. *Believe that, and believe in yourself. Anything is possible.* You can be a star just by living life, enjoying and loving other people, and sharing the spirit that God has for you. It's possible to accomplish your dreams."

As a constant reminder of his greater purpose in life, Derek proudly wears multicolored woven bands on his wrist. On closer inspection the letters stand out: WWJD.

"It stands for What Would Jesus Do?" Derek explains. "A lot of times, sports and athletics are almost barbaric. When

I'm out there competing, it helps me to remember who I am and who I'm out there playing for. I do have a coach. I do have teammates. I do have fans. But ultimately, I'm playing in the name of God."

Derek has someone great as the anchor of his soul. Jesus Christ is in charge of his dream!

What and who is the anchor of your soul? When you embrace Jesus, He will give you a dream, and He will be the anchor of hope that holds through the storms of life. No one illustrates this better than a special friend, Jennifer Rothschild, a woman I admire immensely.

Jennifer grew up in a family of wisdom and faith. That faith enabled her to face darker nights than most can imagine.

At the promising age of fifteen, Jennifer began to suffer from poor vision. Her parents took her for an eye exam. Little did this beautiful, energetic tenth-grade cheerleader know her life was about to change forever. The doctor gave Jennifer and her parents the results of her tests. They discovered that she had a rare disease, retinitis pigmentosa, which was causing her retinas to deteriorate.

Her prognosis was total blindness.

"A silence fell upon the conference room," Jennifer recalls. "I think of what my parents must have been going through on that dark day. No one said anything. That silence followed us as we got into the car and drove home.

"As I was sitting in the backseat of the car, my mind was racing with all the fearful changes and challenges I would now have to face. I remember one of my biggest fears and disappointments was that I was going to miss the ordinary blessings of life. I wasn't going to get to drive a car, and that represented independence. We all feel that if we have wheels, we have wings. I had lots of questions. How will I be able to finish high school and go off to college? Would boys want to date me, and would I get married? How would I take care of children? These were the blessings I was most afraid of losing.

"My father happens to be a pastor—my pastor. It was from him that I learned who God is and how good God is. So I can only imagine what his prayers must have been. I know my mother was heartbroken. I'm sure all of us—father, mother, and teenager daughter—were processing our way through this painful news and praying.

"When we got home, I went in and immediately sat down at our old upright piano. The silence was broken as I played the piano in a way I had never played. I had had a couple of years of lessons, but unfortunately I was not an overly proficient pianist. But that day I began to play by ear. I played a song that I had never played before, and it filled the living room. I do not believe it was an accident. It was the beloved hymn 'It Is Well with My Soul.'

"I know that God, in all of His goodness, had allowed one door to be closed that day at the eye hospital and very mercifully allowed another door to open. The message God spoke to my heart has been the greatest lesson I have ever learned in the dark: it doesn't have to be well with your circumstances for it to be well with your soul."

In the years that followed, Jennifer learned many more lessons in the dark and has been constantly amazed at the hope God has provided. Today she is married to a wonderful man she has never seen, and she is the mother of two boys, fifteen-year-old Clayton and six-year-old Connor, whom she also has never seen. Her eyes, though blind, sparkle and twinkle more than most. Jennifer is the author of several books. She sings, speaks, and inspires people around the country with her gift of wisdom and music. As she says, "Isn't God good? My greatest dream was to be a commercial artist—cartooning, lettering—I thought I was really talented. But God knew that what my eyes could never communicate through visual art, I could now share with the world through the new gift He was giving me: the art of music. So through the gift of music, I can show that it really can be well with your soul.

"Today, twenty-five years later, my disappointments and concerns are different. Sometimes I look at my little children, and I don't see their faces. That is a disappointment. I don't see my husband's face, but I know he is handsome because he tells me he is. But I have found that in what could be a source of great sorrow, God has revealed how amazing His hope is. Sometimes that hope and a bright future just come in a package we didn't anticipate."

Jennifer's solid anchor is Jesus Christ. He has given her a faith to see her through the darkness and to give her hope through despair. And He still fills her life today with the ultimate gift—a beautiful love that this amazing woman found in her family and her faith. A love that she passes on, in joy, to those whose lives she touches.

Love is the last word. The apostle Paul said, "And now abide faith, hope, and love; and the greatest of these is love" (1 Corinthians 13:13).

Without love, faith is unsatisfying.

Without love, hope is joyless.

Without love, ambition is hazardous.

Without love, justice is dangerous.

Without love, suffering is unbearable.

And the love of Jesus Christ is unique. It transcends human love.

It is a divine love on the highest, holiest level.

Self-centered love cries out, "I love you because I want you."

Self-serving love calls out, "I love you because I need you."

Self-giving love reaches out, "I love you because you need me." That's the love that Jesus Christ inspires.

Albert Schweitzer wrote these inspiring words: "I do not know what your destiny will be, but of one thing I can be certain—the only ones among you who will truly be happy are those who sought and found how to serve."

. . .

As I write these words, I have lived through more than four thousand Sundays. There have been very few Sundays that I missed being in church. So for all of my seventy-eight years of life, my weeks started in church, where I was fed with the Spirit of Jesus Christ to inspire me for the next six days. And then, on the next Sunday, I would connect with His Spirit in song and spoken word once again. So for over four thousand Sundays I have been conditioned with an unwavering optimism about my tomorrows. Always I see tomorrow loaded with new dreams and greater possibilities.

I believe in tomorrow because as long as I can remember, these lines have been imprinted on my mind: "I don't know what tomorrow holds, but I know who holds tomorrow."

Yes, God knows more about my tomorrows that I know about my yesterdays.

So I have put the past in its proper place. "I shut the door on yesterday and threw the key away. Tomorrow has no fears for me for I have found today."

I believe in the inevitability of change in life's unfolding process. Life will not be the same tomorrow. I have the freedom to choose to be proactive or reactive as I confront the opportunities that change offers.

I believe in tomorrow because I believe in the positive power of one: one person in the right spot at the right time, and redemption happens.

I believe in the unquenchable human spirit to turn obstacles into opportunities and tragedies into triumphs.

I believe in tomorrow because God is alive. I believe in the universal principle: *Every end is a new beginning.* God transcends death. God is eternal!

I have not changed *the* world, but I have changed *my* world.

Epilogue

I approach the mysterious tomorrow in the same way as I approach an impressive house. I am supposed to call at that intimidating mansion? I walk up the steps. I see the doorbell. I raise my arm. I stretch out my hand. I point my index finger, aiming for the button. I am afraid to touch it. Who is on the other side? A friend or a foe? I pray, "Christ, help me." Now I feel a soft pressure on my elbow, my trembling arm and quivering hand move forward, and the rigid extended finger hits the button. I hear the doorbell ring. I did it. Now the large door moves. It opens, and there stands my best friend, my future. "Welcome. Step in. My name is Tomorrow. How glad I am that you came. Do I ever have some happy surprises for you!" And my tomorrow hugs me. I tremble with the joy of happy expectations. "Thank you, God! You didn't let me throw away my tomorrow."

Acknowledgments

I am deeply grateful foremost to my wife, Arvella, who has edited my messages for over thirty-five years on the *Hour of Power* telecasts and the writing of my many books.

To my daughter, Jeanne Schuller Dunn, who assisted me in organizing my material and compiling the true accounts of my special friends who have inspired me and taught me life's most courageous lessons.

To Barbara Miller who took the hundreds of my handwritten pages and correctly transcribed them to print and computer pages.

To Lois de la Haba, Gideon Weil, and the editors from HarperSanFrancisco who particularly endured my work on this manuscript.

Most importantly, I am deeply grateful for all of the brave and beautiful persons who have allowed me to share their positive stories ...

Renee Bondi, pg. 20
Sue Thomas, pg. 31
Bill Rhodes, pg. 43
Dr. Stephen B. Sample, pg. 46
Millard Fuller, pg. 63. *Bokotola, Love in the Mortar Joints, No More Shacks, The Excitement is Building, More than Houses,*

The Theology of the Hammer, A Simple Decent Place to Live, Building Materials for Life, Volumes I & II

Martin Seligman, pg. 75

A.C. Green, pg. 89. *Victory*

Wayne Gretsky, pg. 93

Evelyn Husband, pg. 98

Erik Weihenmayer, pg. 101. *Touch the Top of the World*

Kathy Ireland, pg. 105. *Powerful Inspiration: Eight Lessons That Will Change Your Life*

Dave Thomas, pg. 107

Lu Ann Mitchell, pg. 119

Gracia Burham, pg. 123. *To Fly Again*

Laura Wilkinson, pg. 129

Col. Norman A. McDaniel, pg. 136. *Yet Another Voice* (Hawthorn Books Inc. 1975)

W. French Anderson, M.D., pg. 174

Derek Fisher, pg. 205

Jennifer Rothschild, pg. 207. *Lessons I Learned in the Dark* (Multnomah), *Touched by His Unseen Hand* (Multnomah), *Walking By Faith* (LifeWay), *Fingerprints of God* (LifeWay)